Praise for *Embracing the Old Witch in the Woods*

"We live in a powerful time in which we need books that remind us of the ancestral, deeply spiritual power that women hold. This book reminds us of that power, and embraces the complexity of what healing might look like. In these pages, Angela J. Herrington dives deep into the patriarchal traps we've fallen into and gives rich steps for us to take in order to rediscover and celebrate the sacred feminine in our lives today. The stories and steps toward empowerment in this book can be life-saving for someone looking to live beyond the toxic power of patriarchy and live into the magic that women hold."

—**Kaitlin B. Curtice**, award-winning author of *Native* and *Living Resistance*

"Practical, insightful, and so necessary, Angela J. Herrington's *Embracing the Old Witch in the Woods: Liberating Feminism from Christian Patriarchy* is required reading for those who grew up in conservative Christian religious traditions, especially women (and those raised as women). If you've been feeling like you're never able to measure up to the standards of society and the church, if you feel like you've been taught not to trust yourself, if you feel like there must be more, this book is for you. Herrington is a gentle and generous guide to unpacking and beginning to heal from harmful gendered messages and embrace a life of fullness and freedom (as well as reclaiming your own inner Old Witch in the Woods)."

—**Shannon T. L. Kearns**, author of *No One Taught Me How to Be a Man: What a Trans Man's Experience Reveals About Masculinity*

"Angela J. Herrington tenderly carries you through learning about the acts of patriarchy to feminine freedom. She reminds us of our own Inner Knowing and invites us to lean into archetypes beyond the maiden. Healing from the Christian patriarchy is no easy feat, yet Herrington creates compassionate space to undo and redo your life beyond religious restrictions. You'll place this book down feeling empowered and POWERFUL."

—**Dr. Candace Linklater**, Indigenous educator and founder of Relentless Indigenous Woman

"Angela J. Herrington's *Embracing the Old Witch in the Woods* is essential reading for anyone who has experienced the impact of anti-woman, patriarchal abuses in organized systems of religion, faith, or spiritual community. Herrington's voice is that of a companion during the often painful process of deconstruction, healing, and finding meaning again after spiritual abuse and religious trauma. The examples offered and stories told are especially relevant to the times in which we find ourselves."

—**Dr. Jamie Marich**, founder of the Institute for Creative Mindfulness, and author of *You Lied to Me About God: A Memoir; Dissociation Made Simple*; and *Trauma and the 12 Steps*

"Angela J. Herrington's refreshing deep dive into feminine wisdom is needed now more than ever. Rather than giving us more rules to follow, she walks with us on a journey out of the lies of patriarchy and into a more authentic, liberated way of living. This is an empowering, inclusive, and freeing read!"

—**Cait West**, author of *Rift: A Memoir of Breaking Away from Christian Patriarchy*

"*Embracing the Old Witch in the Woods* challenges assumptions and norms that are so embedded in our culture that we often don't even see them, even though they impact nearly every facet of our lives and identities. This book will lead you to ask important questions you'll wonder why you never asked before, and will help you see new paths of possibility and promise waiting ahead."

—**Tiffany Yecke Brooks**, bestselling ghostwriter, editor, author, and speaker

EMBRACING THE OLD WITCH IN THE WOODS

ANGELA J. HERRINGTON
FOREWORD BY SHANNON HARRIS

EMBRACING THE OLD WITCH IN THE WOODS

LIBERATING FEMININE WISDOM FROM CHRISTIAN PATRIARCHY

Broadleaf Books
Minneapolis

EMBRACING THE OLD WITCH IN THE WOODS
Liberating Feminine Wisdom from Christian Patriarchy

30 29 28 27 26 25 1 2 3 4 5 6 7 8 9

Library of Congress Control Number: 2025936611 (print)

Cover image: Peter Snayers, The Sonian Forest with travellers on a path, Public Domain
Cover design: Broadleaf Books

Print ISBN: 979-8-8898-3523-3
eBook ISBN: 979-8-8898-3525-7

This book is dedicated to the past, present, and future aunties and grannies. Thank you for your wisdom, fierce heart, and open arms. You will always be the soul fire that helps us compassionately fight the good fight.

And to Sis—You are the best of me, and yet, uniquely yourself. You are the epitome of unconquered feminine fire. I love growing up with you.

Contents

Foreword

As a seven year old in the 1970's, I was curious to understand why it seemed like all my friends and classmates went to church except for me. When I asked my mother about this, she discouraged my questions. She'd experienced a strict Catholic upbringing and had no interest in recreating this life for my brother and me. She wanted me to live guilt free.

In 1996, I was a young, vibrant, college graduate and against my mother's advice, I joined what I thought was a thriving church in the suburbs of Washington, DC. It was the late 1990's and The Purity Movement was in full swing. By marrying one of its most prominent leaders, I secured my fate, and the rest is history. I was a cheery, bright-faced girl who just wanted some religion in her life.

Ten years later, I was a mother of three, a mega-church pastor's wife, homeschooling, entertaining, attending church meetings, and generally working my tail off trying to be a good pastor's wife, a good mother, and a good person, according to the church's definitions for each of these roles. I devoted myself to creating a wholesome, yet idealistic world for my children to enjoy. As they grew, I added homeschooling to my daily duties. If managing three different educations didn't keep me busy enough, as soon as we were finished for the day, there was the mad dash to straighten up, make dinner, or get ready for one of the many evening church meetings that filled our schedule. I'm not sure which was harder, living up to the impossible expectations of others or living up to the impossible expectations I placed on myself.

I know I will never regret the time I spent creating a loving home, or nurturing my children, but I do regret the lack of balance that was my life all those years. I regret the fact that every single bit of my attention went outward and almost none went toward replenishing myself, especially when it is so clear that it would have been better for everyone if I'd been able to prioritize myself more! I regret that it was acceptable for my valuable talents, time, and energy to be used for other people's benefit, financial gain, and growth, but not my own.

I now have the advantage of 20/20 hindsight. Twenty-five years later I know that my religion hadn't given me God, it had given a mandate. "Submit and serve men" was the mandate. I was mined for my resources—my talents, my skills, my energy, my production and re-production value.

It was an unsustainable arrangement, and eventually I had no choice but to break it—I was too exhausted to go further. This was someone else's blueprint for my life, I realized. Someone else had written it. And that someone wasn't anything like me. I needed a better plan, and I needed to connect back to myself again.

I began to overturn beliefs I'd learned. I was not inherently weak and easily deceived, I was intelligent, strong, and capable. I could, in fact, trust myself. I was, in fact, good. I should follow my joy. I started trusting my emotions and attending to my needs. I rekindled my dreams, re-activated my voice, and reclaimed my autonomy. These many different parts of me were my missing pieces!

Angela J. Herrington, having helped many individuals in her coaching practice, and experienced a similar journey herself, understands the significance of these missing pieces, and how critical it is that we correct the hurtful narratives that cause us to lose them generation after generation. She knows that in order to have free, whole, vibrant lives people actually need to be free and whole.

Embracing the Old Witch in the Woods helps us unpack the misunderstandings and false narratives that surround our ideas about femininity; how they were shaped, why they keep us stuck, and where they came from in the first place. Then, after arming us with this powerful knowledge, Angela turns to our attention to more practical matters—reclaiming wholeness in our present lives. It can be lonely, messy work, trying to reclaim a lost self. In uncomplicated terms, *Embracing the Old Witch in the Woods* offers gentle guidance for anyone who is ready to dismantle patriarchy, and looking to reclaim the wholeness and vitality that has always been theirs for the taking. With effortless ease and wisdom, Angela J. Herrington's primer on patriarchy gracefully nudges us toward collective and individual change. A whole and broader view of femininity isn't just for women, and neither is this book—we all need it.

Shannon Harris,
author of *The Woman They Wanted: Shattering the Illusion of the Good Christian Wife*

Introduction

The Witch Trials Never Ended

You've probably seen her in your favorite show, book, podcast, or sermon illustration. The old hag muttering curses as she shuffles about her cottage. The wicked old witch who tries to eat children so she can remain beautiful. The stepmother or mother-in-law with a heart of stone. The power-hungry queen who manipulates her way to the top, only to die violently and be lapped up by wild dogs. The selfish woman who lured her husband into original sin so that she could be like God.

Some are ugly, scarred by time and hard living. Others are beautiful through magic or as a product of their wealth and vanity. They're power-hungry women who resent men, happiness, and anything holy. They're out to harm anyone who crosses their path, and they exude manipulation, dark magic, and bitterness.

We rarely learn about their (perhaps our own) backstory, motivation, or humanity. They become caricatures, standing at the intersection of femininity and malicious intent. Their goal is chaos, retribution, and anything that makes them more powerful. They are dangerous to people we care about (especially the innocent) and society.

These nasty women aren't just historical or literary characters. They are our politicians who push back against cultural norms; survivors of mass gun violence who say "No more!"; community activists who refuse to ignore racism; feminists who fight for gender equity; musicians who are ashamed of a president inciting violence; brilliant first ladies with muscular arms; and yes, even spiritual coaches like me who are calling people out of toxic religious environments.

These characters are the villains of our culture and the warnings of our fairy tales and fables. "Don't be like them!" we are told early and often.

No matter how they're described, the message is clear: Femininity is rooted in evil and needs to be conquered by all means possible. Gender-based hatred, mixed with a hefty dose of white supremacy, colonialism, and toxic religion threatens the lives of millions of women, girls, and nonbinary people around the world.

These narratives about women are not just absurd, they are an insidious form of hate that results in very real harm. It's a harmful narrative that we all internalize, hold ourselves to, and perpetuate on others because we think it is true. The notion that femininity is inherently dangerous—that it must be subdued or controlled—is nothing more than a fabrication born of fear and wielded by systems desperate to maintain their grip on power.

While things have gotten better for white hetero/cis women, more marginalized groups like Black, Indigenous, or other People of Color (BIPOC) and 2SLGBTQIA+ women and femmes, have not historically benefited as much from the fight for equity. The disproportionate burden on BIPOC and 2SLGBTQIA+ women in the fight for equity stems from the intersection of multiple oppressions. These women have often been the backbone of grassroots movements like Title IX (sports equality for girls and women), the right to vote, fair housing legislation, educational equity, and the Equal Rights Amendment. Black women often carry these efforts through their labor, time, money, leadership skills, and wisdom, even while facing systemic inequities. Their lived experiences, shaped by the compounded effects of racism, sexism, and other forms of discrimination, uniquely position them to identify and address injustice.

Yet, the recognition of their contributions remains inadequate, and the benefits of social progress are often unevenly distributed. These communities continuously fight not only for their own survival but for broader societal change, ensuring that the fight for equity includes the most marginalized voices.

When other forms of oppression intersect with gender discrimination, it is always more threatening to BIPOC and 2SLGBTQIA+ women and femmes. Centuries of violence have shaped the expression of their DNA and constantly threaten their well-being. We will talk about how this happens more in chapter 11, but right now it's important to know these threats are not limited to historical cases of persecution, abuse, trafficking, and murder.

The persecution of women that is often called "the witch trials" started well before 1500 and never really ended; it shifted and morphed into different forms, but the vilification of all things feminine is a thread woven throughout our history.

Violence and public persecution intensify when conditions are optimized by rhetoric, religion, and influential people. Thanks to the rising visibility of bigoted leaders, we are currently in one of those flare-ups. The undercurrent of discrimination and resentment has once again risen to the level of a raging river of hate and violence.

Perhaps you picked up this book because you've been overwhelmed by that current and are struggling. Maybe you're sitting on the banks watching loved ones being swept away and feeling tired of feeling helpless. Or perhaps you're just intrigued by the catchy title and snazzy cover design.

No matter how you got here or what you're looking for in these pages, I hope that you'll gain a deeper understanding of the unnatural and unholy vilification of all things feminine. We will spend some time discussing root causes, the cost of not challenging them, and how to untangle yourself from that undercurrent of gender-based bias.

For those directly impacted by the vilification of feminine wisdom, you'll learn to peel back the layers of unhealthy assumptions, beliefs, pressures, and unrecognized self-loathing. For those indirectly impacted, you'll discover that *everyone* is harmed by gender-based hate and violence, including the men who gain power from it. You'll learn to recognize the role you play in a society that glorifies hypermasculine power and how to begin to make things right.

You may be tempted to devour all the words as fast as you can. I get that. I'm a binge reader at heart, but this topic needs time to simmer. If you've been mocked, shamed, or ostracized for your femininity, there's a good chance you'll need space to sit in that grief and care for your tender spaces. I hope you'll extend that grace to yourself.

Holding Space for Grief

If you've been taught that aggression, stoicism, and misogyny are the healthy norm, you're going to need some time to deprogram and adopt new core beliefs. You are going to need space to rage over what was stolen from you and mourn the time and opportunities you can't get back.

It's essential to learn how the vilification of all things feminine shows up in your life, how it harms you, and how you've been taught to harm others with it. All of those things take time, so please don't rush.

It's my hope that you'll approach these ideas with vulnerability, humility, and hope. In order to change, it is important to lower your defenses and acknowledge that the way you know how to exist is not always the best way forward.

Once you stare the root cause of gender-based hardship and trauma in the face, it becomes easier to see exactly what you are responsible for and what responsibility belongs on other people's shoulders. (*Spoiler alert*: It's rarely as much your fault as you've been led to believe.) For the hundreds of women and nonbinary people I've coached, that moment of clarity begins a chain reaction of ever-increasing healing.

The number one thing that I want you to know is you can reject the harmful labels forced upon you by patriarchal society and settle into your truest, most beautiful self. There's liberation in finding out the gender-based curses and flaws you've fought for so long were made up to reinforce an unjust system and have nothing to do with you or the wise women who came before you.

You may even find yourself reaching out to help others who aren't here yet, but the important thing is to put on your oxygen mask and do your own work first. The goodness you find and the love you create within yourself will naturally spill over to the ones you love, your community, and even your descendants who aren't born yet.

How you embrace your wild, sacred, and holy femininity will likely change, and change often creates instability. It may even stir up fear. I hope that during our time together you will begin to trust yourself more deeply and courageously venture into unexplored aspects of your life.

Because that trust is the catalyst to much-needed generational healing that will shift society long into the future.

Chapter 1

The Feminine Wisdom Within

What's the first thing that comes to mind when you hear the phrase "feminine wisdom"? Maybe you think of a loving grandmother who always knows exactly what you need to feel safe or a fierce auntie who steps in to have your back before you even know you need her. Perhaps you envision a passionate activist standing on the front lines, pushing back against unjust systems with unwavering determination. Or maybe your mind goes to the biblical heroines you grew up hearing about—the women who were described as "pure," "loyal," and "pious" as they navigated some of the most traumatic events imaginable, like genocide, sexual assault, and tremendous personal suffering.

If you grew up in a conservative evangelical or fundamentalist Christian environment—or have recently been drawn to the newer TradWives movement—the term "feminine wisdom" might evoke specific images. Perhaps you think of a woman diligently managing her household, nurturing her children, and submissively supporting her husband as an expression of godly femininity. These ideas about "feminine" and "femininity" are shaped by the cultural narratives surrounding us and, for many, those narratives have been tightly controlled by patriarchal teachings that define womanhood in restrictive and limiting ways.

But something crucial is missing from these images of feminine wisdom—something that has been systematically erased by Christian patriarchy for generations: the deep ancestral knowledge that once defined and empowered women. This wisdom, passed down through the generations, isn't just about nurturing or managing a household; it's about understanding our place within the cycles of nature, the spiritual practices that connected us to the earth, and the stories of resilience, survival, and community that shaped our ancestors' lives. Christian patriarchy, through colonization and religious conquest, worked tirelessly to sever these ties, replacing rich ancestral traditions with narrow, Westernized ideals of womanhood.

This disconnection from ancestral wisdom didn't just rob us of valuable knowledge—it disconnected us from ourselves, our communities, and the wisdom of the earth. By demonizing indigenous practices, labeling traditional healers as witches, and replacing matriarchal cultures with patriarchal systems, Christian patriarchy stripped us of the understanding that our feminine wisdom is rooted in something much deeper and more expansive than the roles assigned to us by society. This loss is profound, but recognizing it is the first step toward reclaiming what was taken from us.

In this chapter, we will explore how patriarchal systems—especially those enshrined in Christian doctrine—have distorted and minimized feminine wisdom to consolidate power. But before we dig into that, I want to start by telling you something important: You are not alone in this journey. Whatever feelings of exhaustion, frustration, or even fear that led you here are valid. You may be feeling disconnected from yourself, your body, or the world around you, and that's no accident. Christian patriarchy thrives on disconnection. It has systematically worked to cut you off from the things that make you whole and give you power, and yet, here you are—searching, showing up, seeking something more. That, my dear, takes courage. More courage than you may realize.

In a world that has repeatedly told you that you are not enough—that you need to be more compliant, more beautiful, more silent—simply picking up this book is an act of defiance. It's a signal to the universe that you're ready to take back the parts of yourself that have been hidden, shamed, or silenced. And I want to remind you, before we go any further, that you are enough exactly as you are, in all your complexities and contradictions. The fact that you are here, considering reclaiming your truth, shows me you're already further along this journey than you may think.

The Wicked Woman Trope: How the Vilification of Women's Wisdom Cuts Us Off

The first thing we need to clarify is that this book isn't about teaching witchcraft, a deep-dive into the history of the witch hunts, or how to build houses out of candy to lure unsuspecting children. This book is about reconnecting with the feminine wisdom that has been dismissed, maligned, and even persecuted over the centuries. We are exploring the stories we've been told about women's wisdom, how they've harmed women, and how you can reject those stereotypes to rediscover and reclaim the fullness of who you are.

Let's start with one of the most powerful and damaging stories ever told about women: the trope of the "wicked woman." From Eve in the Garden of Eden to the witches burned at the stake, women's wisdom, intuition, and power have been vilified for centuries. This narrative tells us that if we trust ourselves or follow our desires, we will bring destruction upon the world. How can we possibly connect deeply to a Creator when we've been taught that we, as women, are the reason the world is broken?

But the damage doesn't stop there. The "wicked woman" trope works insidiously, separating us from ourselves at the deepest levels. When we internalize the message that our desires and intuition are inherently flawed, we lose the ability to trust ourselves—not just in spiritual or intellectual matters, but in the most intimate corners of our lives. It creates a disconnection from our bodies, our emotions, and our relationships. It tells us to second-guess our instincts, even in moments when we need them most—like setting boundaries, advocating for ourselves, or making choices about our futures.

By severing this connection to our own wisdom, the trope upholds patriarchal power. A woman who doesn't trust herself is far easier to control. If we are constantly questioning our worth, our judgment, and our abilities, we are less likely to challenge the systems that oppress us. This narrative doesn't just harm women—it maintains the very structures that benefit from keeping women small, silent, and subservient.

On an intimate level, this distrust of ourselves bleeds into our relationships. If we're taught to view our emotions, intuition, and even our own needs as untrustworthy, how can we advocate for ourselves in our partnerships, our friendships, or even in the workplace? How can we claim our voices when we've been told they're inherently dangerous? The trope of the "wicked woman" doesn't just alienate us from power structures—it alienates us from our own inner power and from the sacredness of our lived experiences.

Reclaiming feminine wisdom means rejecting this trope and the control it has exerted for centuries. It means rediscovering that our intuition, our emotions, and our desires are not sources of shame but of profound strength. It means reconnecting to the fullness of who we are and rejecting the lies that have been told about us for generations. In doing so, we don't just heal ourselves—we dismantle the systems that have benefited from our disconnection.

The wicked woman trope isn't just a story—it's a tool. A tool of control used by patriarchal systems to keep women in fear and to make us doubt our inherent power and wisdom. It teaches us that we are not to be trusted, that our instincts and intuition are dangerous. And for generations, this tool has been wielded with ruthless precision, planting seeds of self-doubt and disconnection that grow into barriers between us and our true potential.

Undermining Connection by Cultivating Distrust

For centuries, patriarchal systems have done more than just oppress women—they've taught us to distrust the very things that make us powerful: our intuition, leadership, and emotional depth. This isn't simply about competition among women; it's deeper, running just beneath the surface of our interactions and relationships. Patriarchy conditions us to see feminine wisdom as flawed, unreliable, or weak, and we internalize that belief in ways that quietly undermine our connections to others and ourselves.

Sometimes this internalized distrust surfaces as open competition—a belief that we have to fight for limited spots at the table or that another woman's success somehow diminishes our own. But more often, it shows up in subtler, more insidious ways. For instance, we may find ourselves second-guessing a female colleague's leadership, doubting her ability to make strong decisions or lead effectively. Or we might dismiss another woman's emotional expression as irrational or "too much," mirroring the very stereotypes patriarchy has used to dismiss women for centuries.

This distrust also seeps into how we support—or fail to support—each other. Perhaps you've hesitated to celebrate a friend's success because it triggered feelings of inadequacy. Or maybe you've held back vulnerability with other women, fearing they might judge you or use your honesty against you. These behaviors don't come out of nowhere; they are the echoes of patriarchal messaging that tells us feminine traits, whether in ourselves or others, can't be trusted.

By fostering this quiet mistrust, patriarchal systems ensure that women remain divided and unable to form the kind of bonds that could challenge the status quo. It's not just competition for external approval that keeps us fragmented; it's the unspoken doubts we carry about each other's wisdom and capability, often without even realizing it. By instilling a sense of fear and competition, Christian patriarchy keeps us on edge, guarded, and quick to throw our walls up. It is a huge drain of energy and focus that blocks individual and collective flourishing.

Reclaiming trust in feminine wisdom is not a simple process—it requires unlearning deeply ingrained messages and confronting the ways we've been conditioned to distrust ourselves and others. It's not just about choosing connection over competition; it's about addressing the nuanced and often unconscious ways this distrust has shaped our relationships and perceptions. This type of healing work is complex, uncomfortable, and deeply personal, but it's also profoundly necessary if we hope to create a more equitable, compassionate, and flourishing world.

Defining Feminine Wisdom Beyond the Binary

Feminine wisdom has always existed beyond the rigid, patriarchal gender roles many of us have been taught. Across cultures and history, qualities like intuition, creativity, and compassion have been celebrated as archetypal feminine patterns or energies—universal traits that anyone can embody. Archetypes are powerful because they transcend time, culture, and biology, providing a framework for understanding qualities or roles that exist within all people, regardless of gender. Unlike patriarchal frameworks that falsely tie these traits to biological sex—equating the feminine exclusively with those assigned female at birth and the masculine with those assigned male—archetypes are not linked to genitalia or physical attributes. Instead, they represent energies and qualities that can be expressed by anyone, offering a much more expansive and liberating way to understand humanity.

To understand this balance, think about breathing. Breathing in and breathing out are essential to sustaining life. They are distinctly different in function and appearance—one brings oxygen into the body, while the other releases carbon dioxide—but they work collaboratively to keep us alive and healthy. Feminine and masculine energies work the same way in an equitable society. Each offers something unique, and together they create balance, harmony, and wholeness. Unfortunately, patriarchy pits these energies against one another, teaching us that one is more trustworthy and valuable than the other. This false dichotomy erodes the collaboration between these archetypes and creates systems of imbalance and oppression.

The archetypal feminine includes traits like nurturing, receptivity, emotional intelligence, and relational understanding, while the archetypal masculine encompasses qualities like action, logic, structure, and assertiveness. When allowed to coexist freely, these energies complement each other and enable us to navigate life's complexities. However, patriarchal Christian teachings distorted these archetypes into rigid, gendered roles. This patriarchal distortion redefined feminine traits as inherently belonging to women and masculine traits as inherently belonging to men, tying them to biological sex and using them to justify unequal power dynamics. Men were cast as natural leaders, defined by logic and action, while women were relegated to caregiving roles rooted in submission and service. These roles weren't just restrictive—they became tools of control, stifling the full humanity of all genders.

The harm of this distortion roots itself deep in our identity. For women and anyone embodying feminine traits, it suppresses their wisdom and reduces their contributions to stereotypes of passivity and self-sacrifice. For men, it disconnects them from essential qualities like empathy, vulnerability, and emotional depth by labeling these traits as "feminine" and therefore undesirable. By tying feminine and masculine qualities to rigid definitions of gender, patriarchy erases the rich spectrum of human experience, alienating all of us from our full potential.

While these issues affect everyone, this book centers on the experiences of those most directly impacted by the historical and systemic suppression of feminine wisdom: women and nonbinary folx. This focus does not diminish the harm patriarchal systems have inflicted on men, but here we aim to untangle how these distortions have uniquely oppressed women within patriarchal systems. Healing requires reclaiming both feminine and masculine wisdom in their full archetypal expansiveness, allowing everyone to draw from these energies without fear or shame.

Feminine wisdom isn't confined to nurturing a child or leading a protest—it's about tapping into the creative, intuitive, and relational energy that connects us to ourselves, each other, and the world around us. Reclaiming feminine wisdom isn't about flipping the script to push men to the margins. Instead, it's about dismantling the systems that taught us these traits must compete for power rather than coexist. Archetypes remind us that feminine and masculine energies aren't rivals; they're partners that work together to create balance and wholeness.

By breaking free from binary thinking and rigid roles, we create space for everyone to embrace their full humanity. Feminine wisdom becomes a doorway to deeper connection, healing, and transformation—not just for individuals, but for the systems and societies we live in. This is the kind of world we're working toward—one where we can draw from both feminine and masculine energies freely, allowing everyone to show up as their fullest, most authentic selves.

A Word of Caution Before We Proceed

We need to address a few things before we can have deeper conversations about healing from church-driven misogyny and patriarchal hierarchies. Each of these will be central to decolonizing and stripping away the internalized toxicity of a misogynistic Christian culture.

While it is essential to acknowledge, honor, and learn from traditions devastated by Christian colonization as a step toward collective healing, it is equally important to approach this work with deep respect and humility. Colonial conquest devastated Indigenous communities by stripping them of their resources, disrupting their ability to sustain themselves, and eroding their cultural and spiritual traditions. Colonial powers often imposed European hierarchical structures on these societies, undermining egalitarian systems that had previously supported communal well-being and erasing the wisdom and leadership of women who had played central roles.

Cultural appropriation occurs when individuals or groups adopt elements of another culture, particularly from marginalized communities, without understanding, respecting, or honoring the cultural significance of those practices, symbols, or traditions. For people from dominant cultures—especially white, hetero/cis individuals—this often means taking spiritual or cultural elements from BIPOC communities, stripping away their deeper meanings, and commodifying them for personal gain or superficial use. This act perpetuates the dynamics of colonialism, reinforcing the historical patterns of exploitation and erasure.

Cultural appropriation is harmful because it:

- exploits marginalized communities by commodifying their cultural practices while the communities themselves are often still disenfranchised;

- erases the origins and context of the cultural traditions, reducing sacred practices to trends or novelties;
- reinforces systemic inequalities by benefiting those in privileged positions at the expense of marginalized communities;
- disrespects the spiritual and cultural significance of practices that often hold deep meaning and histories tied to survival, resistance, and identity.

True healing requires dismantling these harmful practices and replacing them with deep respect, genuine understanding, and a commitment to honoring the full depth of these traditions and the communities that sustain them.

The cultural permission for those of us who are white, hetero/cis people to take Indigenous traditions and reframe them for personal or spiritual gain is rooted in the very colonialism we seek to dismantle. For example, using smudging rituals, Indigenous regalia, or spiritual symbols outside of their context not only distorts their meaning but also causes ongoing harm to the communities from which they are taken. Healing cannot come from perpetuating harm; it must come from a place that seeks consent and prioritizes the flourishing of marginalized cultures.

Holding this awareness means resisting the urge to "fix" our own wounds by stealing and polluting what belongs to others. It requires holding space for grief, acknowledging the harm done, and committing to the long, transformative work of mutual respect and reparative justice.

This Isn't the Man-Hater Club

Being pro-woman or pro-feminine wisdom doesn't equate to being anti-men. The idea that supporting women's rights and equity somehow diminishes men is a pervasive myth designed to resist progress. True feminism—and the reclamation of feminine wisdom—is about balance, not revenge. It's about creating a world where everyone, regardless of gender, has the opportunity to live a flourishing life free from oppression.

Imagine the absurdity of saying that for one of your children to thrive, you must oppress and resent your other children. This false dichotomy is rooted in fear, particularly the fear of retribution, and is often weaponized to argue against gender-equity efforts. Feminism, however, is not about flipping the hierarchy but dismantling it entirely, so no one feels the need to suppress or dominate others to feel valued or secure.

Feminine wisdom challenges the rigid structures that have long prioritized dominance and control, calling instead for balance, collaboration, and shared power. Being pro-feminine wisdom doesn't devalue masculine traits; it simply seeks to elevate the traits that have historically been undervalued or dismissed, such as empathy, intuition, and care. This balance benefits everyone because a more equitable world fosters healthier relationships, stronger communities, and fuller lives.

It's also important to recognize that achieving balance doesn't mean giving women identical opportunities to men without addressing the structural inequities of the past. While that approach might seem fair on the surface, it ignores the centuries of oppression, systemic bias, and cultural misogyny that have shaped our current society. Equality doesn't mean starting at the same line when some groups have long been held back; it means providing the resources and support necessary to close the gap.

Healing begins with acknowledging these imbalances and addressing them head-on. It requires us to advocate for systems that uplift all genders, recognizing the need for targeted efforts to empower those who have been historically marginalized. In doing so, we don't just create fairness—we create a world where everyone thrives. Supporting feminine wisdom is not an act of hate or division but a commitment to a shared humanity and a future where equity and dignity are possible for all.

Losing Our Roots

Christian patriarchy didn't just separate us from ourselves and each other; it also severed our connection to our ancestral wisdom—the traditions, practices, and stories that were passed down through generations. Colonization and Christian conquest erased indigenous practices and replaced them with Western Christian ideologies, leaving many of us disconnected from the wisdom of our ancestors.

The systematic disconnection from matriarchal traditions was no accident. Christian patriarchy recognized the threat posed by communities rooted in feminine wisdom, equitable relationships, and earth-based traditions.

During the European witch trials of the fifteenth to eighteenth centuries, women who practiced healing arts, midwifery, and herbal medicine were accused of witchcraft and executed. These women were not just caregivers—they were pillars of their communities, trusted for their knowledge and leadership in health and spiritual matters. Midwives, especially knowledgeable in herbal medicines that reduced pain in childbirth, were seen as heretics because the Catholic Church taught pain in childbirth is God's punishment for Eve's sin.[1] The systematic persecution of midwives and healers destroyed not only individual lives but also the collective wisdom they carried, replacing it with fear and mistrust of feminine knowledge.

In West Africa, colonial Christianity targeted female spiritual leaders such as priestesses, Diviners, and herbalists, labeling them as pagan or demonic. These women were central to the spiritual and social fabric of their communities, and represented a type of gender equity not found in European Christianity.[2] Missionaries and colonial authorities worked to replace their roles with male-dominated Christian hierarchies. This deliberate undermining of women's spiritual authority severed communities from feminine sources of wisdom and disrupted cultural balance.

Similarly, the Highland Clearances in Scotland (the forced displacement of rural populations) dismantled oral traditions and herbal practices often maintained by women. These women carried knowledge of healing and community rituals passed down through generations. When they were uprooted, the cultural and medicinal wisdom they embodied was fractured, and patriarchal norms further discredited their contributions by labeling them as superstitious or backward. The Clearances contributed to the decline of the Gaelic language and associated oral traditions, as communities were dispersed and traditional ways of life were disrupted.

In the Americas, Indigenous traditions were obliterated through forced conversions and missionary schools. Women, who often served as healers, storytellers, and spiritual leaders, were deliberately stripped of their role eliminating their ability to pass on their wisdom. Controlling, traumatizing, and murdering Indigenous women became "a central element in the colonial strategy for conquest and genocide"[3] in Columbus's time. From 1819, institutions like the Carlisle Indian Industrial School in Pennsylvania banned children from learning their own cultural and spiritual practices—many of which were traditionally passed down by women—and replaced them with male-led Christian ideologies.[4] This systematic erasure decimated the feminine wisdom that had been the backbone of these societies.

The impact of these atrocities was devastating for everyone, but the deliberate targeting of women as carriers of cultural, spiritual, and medicinal wisdom contributed to a profound disconnection from feminine knowledge. Christian patriarchy didn't just suppress women; it severed entire communities from the feminine traditions that grounded them, leaving a legacy of fear and mistrust of feminine wisdom that persists today.

But our roots, our connection to ancestral wisdom, are still there. We can reclaim them, and in doing so, we can reclaim parts of ourselves that we may have thought were lost forever. Reclaiming ancestral wisdom is about honoring the stories, practices, and rituals that were silenced. It's about recognizing that the wisdom we need to live fully and freely isn't lost—it's waiting for us to remember, to reconnect.

The power of storytelling and remembering cannot be overstated. When we remember, we heal. And when we heal, we empower ourselves and the generations that will come after us. The stories and practices that once connected women to the earth, to the sacred, and to each other are still alive in us. They may be buried deep beneath layers of patriarchal conditioning, but they are there, waiting to be uncovered, waiting to be lived out in new and meaningful ways.

Finding a Reason to Fight for Yourself

Millions of women are fighting this same battle against patriarchy, and it may surprise you that I'm not going to share their stories in this book. That's intentional. Why? Because when you're untangling yourself from patriarchy, it's easy to get caught up in comparing your story to others. The hard truth is that most of us have been taught to seek external validation. We've learned to be inspired by others hitting the goals or making the changes we long to make. But inspiration alone isn't enough.

In the classic hero's journey that we see in movies and books, the hero doesn't know they're a hero until someone else tells them. They fight a bad guy and eventually learn to trust themselves. While it's a compelling narrative, it's based on external motivation. But if you really want to reject what

Christian patriarchy has said about you, your motivation has to come from within.

There may be external events that contribute to your journey—shared wisdom, collective experiences, or insight from a trusted friend—but today, in this moment, the motivation has to come from inside you. The truth is, no one else's story matters when it's *your* inner story we're rewriting. As long as you're tangled up in Christian patriarchy, other people's stories will always be filtered through that lens. The hardest thing you may ever do is pull away from external validation. Other people's stories may inspire or discourage you, but what will change your life is tuning into your own desire for transformation.

Healing Through Reconnection

This is your personal invitation to reject whatever shamefulness or negativity you've been taught about yourself. I'm not here to give you permission—seeking permission would just be more of that external validation we're trying to move away from. Instead, I'm here to walk you through what I've seen work for hundreds of women who were overwhelmed and exhausted by it all. My hope is that by the end of this book you'll have a deeper understanding of how this kind of oppression has trampled on so many parts of you. The reason I work with women like you is because it can take years to fully comprehend just how insidious Christian patriarchy is. There are things we do and feel every day that are 100 percent related to the lies we were told about feminine wisdom, bodies, and abilities.

I hope that when you finish this book, you'll say, "I didn't even know that was in there," because we're about to do some deep digging. Together, we will heal by reconnecting—with ourselves, with each other, and with the wisdom that patriarchy has tried to erase. You've already taken the first step just by being here. Now, let's keep going.

What I'm proposing here is not Joseph Campbell's hero's journey, where the focus is on conquering or banishing foes. Those stories are always kicked off by an outside force—some external "bad guy" it's easy to identify and hate. That's a method of othering that only creates more resentment and angst.

Instead, I'm inviting you on a healing journey rooted in mothering yourself, your loved ones, and your greater community. There are certainly going to be "bad guys" everywhere, but in this season, your journey is about understanding how you've been taught to live in their shadows. Once we've identified those limiting beliefs, internalized misogyny, and tender spaces that didn't get what they needed to feel safe, we can tap into the deep well of self-healing and nurturing ourselves. It's a journey of self-mothering and learning how to root our inner language in trauma-informed compassion.

I want to be clear: Just as we expanded the definition of feminine wisdom above, I'm talking about an expansive definition of mothering, too. This is not mothering in the patriarchal, colonized sense, which emphasizes cooking, cleaning, and raising children (though some of us will do those things, as well). I'm talking about mothering in an archetypal sense—rooting yourself deeply in a soulful mothering that stands in direct opposition to the hero's journey. You don't have to go anywhere to seek adventure; you are going within to discover what is already there. This soulful mothering is a practice and a posture that recognizes every human has the capacity for creating healing out of nothing more than their own soul.

It's a journey that holds space for all the seasons and stages of life without forcing them into linear narratives or contemporary cultural expectations. It also eliminates the reliance on unnatural binary gender definitions by releasing us from the hypermasculine and submissive feminine roles pushed by patriarchal religions.

By embracing this mothering journey, we can reclaim our sacred and God-given wisdom, create real change, and build a world where every person can stand in their truth, honor their gifts, and lead with the strength that has always been theirs.

So, how do we do that? It all begins with turning the page and diving into the next chapter, where we'll untangle the power of embodiment from Christian patriarchy and begin reclaiming the wisdom of living fully within our own bodies.

Chapter 2

Bodies

We have to start our rejection of Christian patriarchal oppression of all things feminine by literally taking a long, hard look in the mirror at our bodies. Bodies, in general, but especially female and nonbinary bodies, have been blamed for everything from men's inability to control their sexual urges to the entry of evil into the world (and, therefore, all subsequent suffering).

Our culture at large bombards us with messages that associate bodies, particularly feminine bodies, with shame and inadequacy. However, for those raised within or near Christian patriarchy—most often in conservative and fundamentalist church communities—these cultural pressures are intensified. These environments layer on a uniquely oppressive burden through shame-based teachings about bodies, sexuality, and self-expression. It's a double dose of negativity: one from general societal standards and another, perhaps more sinister, from spiritualized moral expectations.

How in the world are you supposed to achieve the perfect body, home, and faith while remaining modest, humble, and putting everyone else first? Many don't realize how those teachings impact things we would never think are related to our body image. For example, if women are "supposed" to be submissive because our hearts are sinful and our desires are lust-filled, how does that impact our ability to ask for what we deserve at work, at home, and in our most intimate relationships? If our bodies are filled with broken and sinful thoughts, how does that impact our ability to trust our intuition and set healthy boundaries?

We will dive into each of those topics in upcoming chapters, but first, let's unpack this whole idea that our bodies, specifically women's bodies, are untrustworthy and never seem to be good enough.

The very first step of this unpacking is to ask: Has it always been this way? Were women's bodies always seen as something to be controlled and suppressed? Not exactly.

What Christian Patriarchy Says About Our Bodies

Prebiblical and Biblical Views on Bodies

Many cultures revered the female body even before the biblical era. Goddesses were worshipped as symbols of fertility, wisdom, and strength. The body, especially the woman's body, was seen as a source of life and connection to the Divine. In ancient civilizations like Mesopotamia and Egypt, women had roles as priestesses and healers. Their bodies were seen as vessels of power, not something to be feared or controlled.

But other early texts paint a different picture. Women like Eve, often portrayed as the first to sin, started to symbolize temptation and humankind's "fallen nature." The story of Eve in the Garden of Eden is the cornerstone of Christian patriarchy's argument that women's bodies are untrustworthy, sinful, and need to be disciplined.

But even in biblical texts, the view of bodies wasn't entirely negative. The *Song of Solomon* celebrates the beauty and sensuality of the human body, showing that not all views of female sexuality were rooted in shame in ancient Israel. However, the seeds of control had been planted, and as Christianity developed, these ideas became more deeply entrenched.

Pushing Goddesses Aside to Promote Patriarchy

In many ancient societies, goddesses like Isis, Inanna, and Artemis were central to spiritual and cultural life, symbolizing power, fertility, and protection. For many, the female body itself was seen as a sacred vessel of divine strength and creation. The Canaanite pantheon included Asherah, a goddess sometimes regarded as Yahweh's consort in early Israelite religion.[1] This balance of divine male and female figures mirrored early human relationships and upheld a vision of the universe where masculine and feminine forces were equally revered.

However, as monotheistic Yahwism established itself, these divine feminine figures were intentionally diminished. Then, once Christianity began to spread—especially after its adoption as the dominant religion of the Roman Empire—goddess worship was not merely dismissed, it was suppressed to promote a patriarchal framework. It was no longer acceptable for goddesses to coexist with a male god. Instead, power and divinity became exclusively associated with masculinity. The church began recasting the female body as weak, sinful, and in need of control, transforming the reverence once held for feminine deities into suspicion and fear.

This shift was not merely a move from polytheism to monotheism but from a belief system where male and female deities held balanced, co-ruling power to one where a solely male deity reigned. In early traditions, godly pairs, like the god El and goddess Asherah, represented a harmonious duality, embodying a model of equality. This pairing paralleled the creation story of Adam and Eve, where two figures were designed to coexist, complementing one another. However, as monotheism evolved, Yahweh's status as the singular male deity took precedence, and any associated goddesses were erased or rebranded as idols.

This shift wasn't just theological; it was political. By demonizing or erasing goddesses, the church reinforced the idea that men were divinely appointed to lead while women were meant to follow. Women's bodies, once celebrated as sacred vessels of life and wisdom, were recast as temptations and sources of sin. Goddess worship, which had once empowered women and connected them to the Divine, was replaced by a patriarchal narrative that emphasized women's inferiority and the need for their bodies to be controlled.

As the religion pushed these goddesses aside, it cast their wisdom, and the wisdom of the women who followed them, into the shadows. Like the old witch in the woods, these female deities—who once held the power of life, healing, and connection to the Divine—were recast as dangerous threats to the established order. Their knowledge was no longer revered; it was feared.

Mary and the Pure Woman

Let's talk about Mary—the ultimate figure of womanhood in Christian tradition. For her to be venerated, she had to be extraordinary. Early church fathers consistently depicted Mary as the ultimate model of purity and submission, elevating her as the ideal woman within Christian tradition. Early church fathers like Augustine reinforced this depiction,[2] highlighting her purity as her defining characteristic.

Similarly, Ambrose presented Mary's life as a template for all women, stating, "Mary's life should be for you a pictorial image of virginity. Her life is like a mirror reflecting the face of chastity and the form of virtue. Therein you may find a model for your own life . . . showing what to improve, what to imitate, what to hold fast to."[3]

Jerome reinforced this narrative by tying Mary's worthiness as the Mother of God directly to her virginity, writing, "She was chosen to be the Mother of the Lord, and to remain a virgin."[4] These portrayals of Mary focus not on qualities like wisdom or strength, but on her obedience to divine will and her willingness to relinquish agency over her body. Through these teachings, the church established Mary as the epitome of feminine virtue, contrasting her purity and submission with the supposed sinfulness and danger associated with other women.

But here's the kicker: Mary's purity and submission weren't just used to tell her story—they were also used to point out how much the rest of us fall short. She was elevated as the ideal woman not because she was strong, wise, or independent, but because she was obedient. She willingly gave up control of her body, quite literally, to serve God's plan.

That's what made her worthy of honor: her submission and her willingness to let go of any personal agency to please God.

Now, contrast that with how the rest of us have been portrayed. The rest of womankind had to be cast in a villainous light to elevate Mary as extraordinary. There needed to be an anti-Mary, or her submission was nothing special. We weren't seen as pure, trustworthy vessels; we were sinful, seductive, and dangerous. Our bodies, unlike hers, were a problem. The church needed a contrast: Mary's pure submission versus the sinful nature of all other women.

From there, it's easy to see how this story of the "pure" woman took root in Christian tradition. Mary was the exception, and the rest of us? We were the rule. Our bodies were inherently flawed, meant to be controlled, hidden, and restrained. This narrative, reinforced for centuries, laid the groundwork for what eventually became purity culture.

The Church's Role in Shaping Attitudes About Bodies

As Christianity grew, teachings about the body became more restrictive. Many of the early church fathers, like Augustine and Jerome, were instrumental in shaping a view of the body deeply tied to sin. Augustine, for example, linked bodily desires, especially sexual lust, to the transmission of original sin from generation to generation. He taught that the body was weak and corruptible, always pulling us toward sin unless we brought it under control through discipline and abstinence. It's also notable that when describing lust and the transmission of sin, Augustine uses female pronouns. He stated carnal concupiscence (the tendency of humans to lust[5]) was both the "daughter of sin" and, when acted upon, the "mother of many sins" that transmits it to the next generation.[6]

These ideas were woven into the fabric of Christian teaching and, over time, they solidified the belief that the body—particularly the female body—was dangerous and needed to be subdued. It wasn't just about individual piety; it became a broader societal expectation. Women's bodies were either pure, like Mary's, or they were temptations, like Eve's. And there was little room for anything in between.

When patriarchal messages about our bodies and our worth are absorbed from such a young age, they start to shape everything we do. It's like living with a filter that distorts how we see ourselves and the world around us. The worst part? We often don't even know it's happening.

This internalization shows up in the smallest details of daily life—whether it's feeling the need to apologize for taking up space, doubting our worth when we don't meet impossible beauty standards, or fearing judgment when we express our desires. These reactions are the result of years of absorbing the idea that we are the problem, that our bodies are the problem, and that we need to control and contain ourselves to be acceptable.

Purity Culture's Legacy of Shame

Fast forward to the twentieth century, and the emergence of purity culture within Evangelical Christianity reignited many of these old ideas. Suddenly, entire movements were built around controlling women's bodies, teaching young girls that their worth was tied to their ability to remain "pure" until marriage. This wasn't new, but it was a modern repackaging of long-standing teachings that told women their bodies were a problem to be managed, not a source of power or wisdom.

Purity culture doubled down on the idea that women's bodies were inherently dangerous, especially to men. The responsibility for men's actions, their lust, and their lack of control was placed squarely on the shoulders of women. We were told to cover up, to behave modestly, to be quiet and submissive so that we wouldn't "tempt" the men around us.

Purity culture's legacy of shame isn't just about controlling women's bodies—it's about keeping women disconnected from themselves. When we are taught to distrust our own desires, we are cut off from the very source of our power. Patriarchy thrives on this disconnection because it ensures we remain divided—from ourselves, from our bodies, and from each other.

But purity culture isn't confined to the church. It seeps into every aspect of life, from how we dress to how we interact with men in the workplace. The idea that our bodies are objects to be controlled has become so normalized that many of us internalized these beliefs without even realizing it.

Purity culture's grip on our bodies doesn't loosen easily. Even for those of us who have left the church or deconstructed our faith, the shame it instilled can linger. We internalize the message that our bodies aren't good, pure, and worthy of love unless they conform to a very specific standard.

And that standard is impossible. It demands that we be pure, chaste, and attractive enough to secure a husband. It tells us to be thin (but not too thin), modest (but not too modest), beautiful (but not to other men), and desirable (but not desiring). We were set up to fail, and the guilt and shame that come with that failure have followed many of us into adulthood.

Disability, Physical, and Mental Illness Under Christian Patriarchy

Christian patriarchy doesn't stop at prescribing narrow ideals for feminine bodies; it also upholds damaging standards for physical, mental, and emotional wellness. Disabled bodies of every gender—whether visibly different or functioning in "nonnormative" ways—are often pitied, stigmatized, or viewed as "broken" and in need of "healing." This insidious attitude extends to those living with chronic illnesses or mental health challenges. Rather than honoring the reality and resilience of living with these conditions, Christian patriarchy often regards such conditions as moral failings, punishments, or states to be "overcome" in order to be considered "whole."

For those with mental or chronic illnesses, this narrative is uniquely isolating. Instead of recognizing these conditions as valid expressions of human diversity, patriarchal systems label them as signs of weakness, sin, or even evidence of lacking faith. People facing mental health challenges or chronic pain are often encouraged to "pray away" their symptoms, implicitly suggesting that their suffering is spiritual rather than physical or psychological. This can drive individuals to internalize blame and disconnect from their bodies, rather than seek the support and care they need.

It's important to reject these harmful narratives, which perpetuate the idea that health issues, disabilities, infertility, and miscarriages are punishments for personal failings or sins. John 9:2–3 challenges this perspective when Jesus responds to a question about a man's blindness: "*Neither this man nor his parents sinned.*" This scripture refutes the notion that physical conditions are tied to moral failure, reminding us that suffering is not divine retribution.

Moreover, mental illness, substance-use disorders, and disordered eating have physiological and systemic components that make them far more complex than simple "consequences of personal decisions." These issues are influenced by genetics, environment, trauma, and societal pressures, dismantling oversimplified narratives of individual blame.

Christian patriarchy dehumanizes people by denying the inherent wisdom and worth within their unique experiences.

Disabled bodies, those living with chronic illness, and those navigating mental health challenges possess deep reserves of strength, adaptation, and insight—qualities that patriarchal systems often overlook. These individuals hold invaluable perspectives on resilience, self-care, and navigating a world that rarely meets their needs. Yet patriarchal Christianity reinforces the toxic narrative that only "able" bodies and minds are valuable, keeping entire communities marginalized and unseen.

We must also acknowledge that the inequities people with disabilities and others face are exacerbated by living in an imbalanced, capitalist society that places undue pressure on the most marginalized while stripping away their resources through predatory practices. Physical, emotional, financial, relational, and spiritual resources are not equitably distributed, and these systemic injustices create barriers that limit access to care and opportunities to thrive.

While I promise these things *should be* our birthright, I also recognize the immense disparities in access to what we need for flourishing. Flourishing isn't about achieving perfection or conforming to harmful standards; it's about creating a society that supports the dignity and value of every person, regardless of ability or circumstance.

Which brings us to the next question: If we've spent our whole lives being told our bodies are the problem, what's the truth about our bodies outside of Christian patriarchy?

What's True About Bodies?

Here's the truth: Your body is good. Full stop. She's not something to be controlled, hidden, or fixed. She's something to be loved, cherished, and honored. When we step outside of Christian patriarchy, we begin to see our bodies for who they really are—powerful, intuitive, and deeply connected to who we are at our core. Our bodies aren't something separate from us—they *are* us. And they're trustworthy.

One of the most radical shifts we can make is to stop seeing our bodies as the enemy. For so long, we've been told that our desires, needs, and even our physical appearance are things to be controlled, denied, or suppressed. But when we look beyond the teachings of purity culture, we start to realize that our bodies are full of wisdom.

Think about how often you feel things in your body before you even understand them. That gut feeling when something is off. That sense of peace when you're in the right place at the right time. Our bodies know things. They've been trying to tell us for years, but we've been taught not to listen.

Redefining Our Relationship with Our Bodies

Christian patriarchy teaches us to divide bodies into "good" and "bad." The "good" bodies are pure, modest, and controlled, while the "bad" bodies are lustful, sinful, and out of control. But that binary is a lie. First of all, who gets to draw the line between in control and out of it? More importantly, every body, no matter her size, shape, ability, or age, is good. There is no one way to have a "good" body. The only thing your body needs to be is yours.

This binary thinking is pervasive in our society. We see it in diet culture, fitness culture, and even in expectations placed on mothers. We're constantly told our bodies must look or behave a certain way to be worthy of love, respect, or care. But the truth is, your body is worthy simply because she exists.

The Dove Global Beauty and Confidence Report reveals that 85 percent of women and 79 percent of girls feel body-related anxiety that prevents them from participating in activities and fully living their lives.[7] This demonstrates the devastating impact patriarchal teachings have and highlights the urgent need to reclaim our bodies.

But what are we replacing this binary thinking with? If we're no longer judging our bodies as good or bad, what do we choose to see instead? We replace it with truth. The truth is that your body is not something to be ranked, judged, or defined by external standards. Instead of asking ourselves if our bodies are "good enough," we begin asking questions like:

- *What do I need?*
- *What is my body telling me?*
- *How can I honor my body today?*
- *How can I work with my body today instead of exploiting it?*

We reject Christian Patriarchy by replacing judgment with curiosity. Instead of categorizing our bodies as good or bad based on external appearance or behavior, we start to approach our bodies with the understanding that they are a fundamental part of our humanity. Our bodies are not passive objects—they are active participants in our lives, full of wisdom and intuition. They are guides, teaching us through feelings, sensations, and needs.

When we reject the dichotomy of good versus bad, we open ourselves up to a relationship with our bodies based on respect and care rather than shame and control. We begin to ask how we can nurture and support our bodies rather than diminish and constrain them. This shift allows us to tap into the body's inherent resilience and strength, recognizing that its needs, desires, and imperfections are not flaws but parts of what make her—and us—whole.

Instead of the harmful binary, we embrace an idea of wholeness—acknowledging that our body's worth is inherent, that she is good and strong not because she fits a particular mold but because she is alive and an essential part of us. Even in the midst of chronic illness, mental health battles, and disability, our bodies deserve to be honored for being present in whatever state is possible. This means letting go of perfection and instead focusing on partnership. Our body is not something to be controlled but a collaborator in our well-being.

It's important to acknowledge that embracing our bodies in this way doesn't mean spiritually bypassing the very real suffering we might experience. Pain, grief, rage, or frustration about our bodies' conditions and functionality are valid and deserve space to be felt. Reconnection to our bodies doesn't ask us to ignore these realities but instead encourages us to remain present with them. In the midst of chronic illness, mental health struggles, or physical limitations, staying connected to our bodies allows us to honor their ongoing efforts and their role in our lives, even when they aren't functioning as we'd hope.

Your body isn't the enemy; she's the ally you always wanted but maybe never realized you had access to. So, let's learn how to reconnect with her. Reconnection begins by reframing how we see our bodies and rejecting the messages that taught us they were dangerous or defective. We can turn to other perspectives, such as those in Indigenous and nonpatriarchal communities, that celebrate the body as sacred, strong, and integral to our wholeness. In many traditions, the female body symbolizes life, wisdom, and resilience, not something to be hidden or controlled.

Embracing the Body's Wisdom and Resilience

What does it mean to embrace this new way of thinking? It means understanding that our bodies carry stories, emotions, and memories that are vital to our growth. The aches, the tension, the cravings—all of it is communication from your body. When we stop silencing those messages and start listening, we gain access to a deeper level of self-awareness and healing.

The trauma many of us carry from these teachings is real, but here's the good news: your body knows how to heal. She's been carrying you through every moment of shame, fear, and judgment, and she's still here—still capable of joy, pleasure, and connection. Still capable of healing.

And bodies of Black and Brown women have endured even greater harm under systems of patriarchy, colonization, and slavery. The great suffragist and former enslaved woman Sojourner Truth spoke directly to this reality in her famous 1851 speech, "Ain't I a Woman?" She highlighted the labor her body performed in fields, enduring alongside men without the luxury of help or protection afforded to white women. Truth's words remind us that these narratives of bodily fragility are not only harmful but also deeply rooted in racial and patriarchal oppression. They erase the strength and wisdom carried in the bodies of women who have long borne the weight of inequity, labor, and resilience.

Historical evidence and research show how resilient women's bodies are. In many preindustrial societies, women engaged in substantial physical labor, often performing tasks comparable to those of men. For instance, in various horticultural and agrarian communities, women were primarily responsible for crop cultivation. A study analyzing the division of labor across different societies found that in 72 percent of horticultural societies and 41 percent of agrarian societies, women were the main contributors to heavy agricultural work.[8] These insights directly challenge the patriarchal narrative of weakness and demonstrate that our bodies are designed to endure, nurture, and thrive.

Our bodies are not fragile, nor are they problems to be solved. They are powerful, dynamic, and adaptive. Embracing this truth is key to unlearning the damaging dichotomy of good versus bad bodies and beginning the journey toward a relationship built on respect, care, and trust.

When we honor our bodies and the resilience they carry—whether through the stories of our foremothers or our own lived experiences—we reclaim the power patriarchy tried to suppress. This reclamation is not just an act of healing for ourselves; it's an act of honoring the women who came before us and empowering those who will follow. Our bodies are more than enough—they always have been.

The First Step Toward Loving Every Inch of You

It may seem oversimplified, but the key to rejecting Christian patriarchal teachings about bodies is to push back against the voices that have hammered us with harmful messages for years. In their place, we need to create space for self-compassion, curiosity, and grief for what has been lost along the way. Healing begins when we acknowledge the impact these teachings have had on our relationship with our bodies, and we start the journey back to reclaiming what was always ours: the inherent goodness of our physical selves.

For many of us, our bodies have become something we manage, manipulate, or even despise—beings we constantly criticize or ignore. We start referring to our body as "it," as if our body is somehow separate from who we truly are. We say things like "I need to get my body into shape," treating our bodies as something outside of ourselves rather than a part of our whole being. My friend Lisa calls it living in a "meat suit"—just dragging around a body while the "real" us does the thinking, feeling, and living.

But here's the thing: This language, this separation, is the first step in dehumanizing ourselves. When we reduce our bodies to an "it," we start to judge them more harshly. We treat them as disposable, temporary beings that get in the way instead of integral parts of who we are.

This split is not just emotional—it's spiritual. It's how Christian patriarchy thrives, teaching us that our bodies are sinful, shameful, and in need of control.

Words Matter: Changing How We Speak About Our Bodies

For centuries, women's bodies—much like the old witch in the woods—have been described in ways that paint them as dangerous, unruly, and in need of control. But just as the witch's wisdom holds power, so too does the language we use to reclaim our bodies. By speaking of our bodies with reverence and respect, we challenge the narratives that have been used to diminish our power.

Your body is a part of your humanity as much as your thoughts, emotions, and spirit. When we talk about our bodies as separate entities, we lose touch with what it means to be whole, embodied beings. And when we view our bodies through this fragmented lens, we can't fully connect with ourselves or others.

So, how do we start reclaiming our bodies? How do we move past the language that reduces them to objects and begin to see them as sacred again? The first step is to change how we talk about our bodies. You are not somehow separate from your body. When you feel tired, *you* are tired, not just your body. When you need care, *you* need care. You deserve to experience pleasure, joy, rest, and everything your body is capable of offering. By changing the language, we begin to reintegrate our bodies into our sense of self and heal the wounds caused by years of internalized objectification.

Healing the Fractured Relationship with Our Bodies

At first, it may feel awkward or forced, but words hold immense power. Referring to your body respectfully and using words affirming your humanity is a small yet transformative step toward reclaiming her. Your body isn't an "it"—she's a "she," a "they," or even a "we." She's not a suit you wear or a tool you use—she's you. Treating your body as part of your full human self is the foundation of healing from years of internalized shame and detachment.

For so long, we've been taught to "other" parts of ourselves—to see our bodies as separate from our minds, hearts, and souls. Christian patriarchy thrives on this division. It's why we've been made to feel like our bodies don't truly belong to us, like they're something to be managed, controlled, or fixed. But the path to healing lies in mending that fractured relationship and reclaiming our bodies as sacred, whole, and worthy of care and respect.

When we are taught to "other" our bodies, it can feel like we're living in pieces—our thoughts and emotions disconnected from the physical vessel that carries us through the world. This disconnection creates shame, frustration, and a lack of trust in ourselves. We're convinced there's a war between our desires and morals, physical needs and spiritual worth. And that's how patriarchy keeps us small.

But the only way to heal from this is to reclaim our bodies as part of our whole self. It means letting go of constant judgment and allowing ourselves to be curious, to listen to what our bodies have been trying to tell us all along. Your body holds memories, wisdom, and intuition. She's not a separate, sinful part of you but, rather, the key to understanding and healing. When you stop treating your body as something separate, you begin to see the beauty in your wholeness.

When we begin to heal the fractured relationship with our bodies, we are no longer afraid of the power our bodies hold, no longer willing to let patriarchal systems define us as dangerous or out of control. Just like the old witch in the woods who lives outside of patriarchal culture's expectations, we reclaim our full, embodied selves—the wisdom and strength that have always been within us.

Wholeness Is Worth the Fight

This integration journey isn't always easy, but it's the only way to live fully. Walking as a whole being means acknowledging that your body isn't broken, sinful, or an obstacle to be overcome. She's a sacred part of you. When you integrate body and soul, when you stop treating them as separate entities, you'll begin to trust yourself more deeply, honor what your body tells you, and release the shame that's been weighing you down for so long.

When you mend your relationship with your body, you stop treating her like something external that needs fixing. Instead, you see her as an extension of your spirit—powerful, worthy, and whole. And when you embrace your body as an integral part of yourself, you start to move through the world as a complete, empowered person—no longer fragmented but fully, truly whole.

Leaning In: Turning Inward

There are many activities that teach you how to connect with your body, (you can find some here https://angelajherrington.com/connect-with-your-body) and they're great, but I want to take it one step further and teach you how to have a two-way conversation with your body.

You'll begin by settling into your body and turning your focus inward to listen, observe, and hold space for yourself. We will refer back to this posture over and over again as centering or anchoring in your body. It's perfectly normal for this to be challenging, especially if you've never been taught how to shut out external voices and tune into your body. When I first tried, my body was so noisy with unresolved trauma, worries, and chatter that it sounded like Times Square during rush hour!

The most important thing is to not judge or shame yourself for feeling awkward or not producing the results you think you "should" have achieved. That's the old patriarchal, capitalist way of thinking that says you need to produce for something to be worthwhile. This journey is about listening to your body, recognizing her wisdom, and discovering what she has to share with you. This activity is about experiencing your body, not producing a certain result.

You're learning to trust yourself in new ways, and that can be really hard, but keep trying. It helps to tie this experience to certain smells and sounds. Create a routine by sitting in the same location, lighting a candle, and listening to quiet music that supports your journey. I've created a few playlists at angelajherrington.com/playlists to help you get anchored in your body during this practice, but remember, you don't have to use them. Do what helps you be most present.

Step 1: Create Space for Yourself

Grab a journal and something to write with and find a quiet, comfortable space. Settle into a position where you feel fully supported, whether sitting or lying down. Shut off your notifications, and tell others you don't want to be disturbed for at least half an hour. Take a few slow, deep breaths, feeling the rise and fall of your chest. Allow the weight of your body to relax into the surface beneath you.

Step 2: Lean Into Your Rhythm

As you breathe, begin to notice the natural rhythm of your body and how she feels in this moment. Focus solely on your breathing and imagine every inhale going a bit deeper into your body. Let each breath fill your chest and expand your belly. Take a few minutes to settle into your body and let her know you are ready to listen.

Step 3: Notice What You Feel

When you feel settled in, notice the parts of your body that feel different. Is there an area of tension? Pain? Numbness? Pick a single area to focus on for this activity. The goal is a two-way conversation, but those don't always make sense, especially when this process is new. This is your chance to observe without judgment and listen to what your body tells you at each stop.

Step 4: Curiously Observe

Take a few moments to observe what's there (without judgment) and ask yourself one or more of these questions:

- *What's going on here?*
- *What do you want me to know?*
- *What do you need from me right now?*
- *How can I support you?*

Remember, there are no right or wrong answers. This activity is solely for the purpose of curiously connecting with our bodies. Be sure to continue your deep breathing as you listen.

Step 5: Note Your Observations

When you sense there is nothing else to say right now, thank your body for what she's shared with you, even if it's messy or unclear. Take a few moments to jot down what you experienced in a journal or notebook. Be careful not to filter, rationalize, or dismiss anything from this experience.

Once you've captured your thoughts, ask your body one more time what she needs right now to feel cared for, and then go grab a nourishing snack, take a walk, rest for a bit, or do some stretching. Be sure to thank your body for the insight she has just offered you.

Repeat this activity several times each week while you're working through this book. Implementing it as a daily practice would be very impactful, but don't pressure yourself or slip into perfectionism. Be patient and real with yourself. A new practice done consistently a few times a week is better than shaming yourself into daily sessions where you just go through the motions.

Congrats! You just took the first step toward rejecting the vilification of your own body and inner wisdom. Let's take that embodied connection into the next chapter and talk about how to heal our tender spaces within.

Chapter 3

Mothering

In her book *Of Woman Born*, Adrienne Rich said something that really sticks with me: "The institution of motherhood is not identical with bearing and caring for children, any more than the institution of heterosexuality is identical with intimacy and sexual love."[1] It's such a simple statement, but it opens up a whole new way of thinking about motherhood. For so long, we've been taught that motherhood is this rigid role—something that demands obedience, sacrifice, and losing yourself. But what if we saw mothering differently? What if it were less about rules and expectations and more about creativity, love, and power?

Let's be real: The way patriarchal religion has defined mothering hasn't done us any favors. It tells us our worth comes from how much we can give to others, how many kids we have, or how much of ourselves we're willing to sacrifice in the name of being "good." And if you're like me, you've felt the weight of that. It's suffocating, isn't it? Like there's this impossible standard we're all supposed to meet, and no matter how hard we try, it's never enough.

The problem is that so many of us have been handed this version of motherhood that asks us to disappear. Being a "good" mom, we're told, means putting everyone else first, all the time, with no room for what we want or need. It's exhausting. No wonder so many of us feel disconnected from the joy and creativity that mothering could bring.

But what if mothering wasn't about that? What if it was something we got to define for ourselves? What if it became an act of choice—where we decide what it means to create and nurture life, how we want to show up, and how we heal ourselves and others, all without the weight of these outdated expectations dragging us down?

That's what we're here to figure out together. In this chapter, we're going to unpack how toxic religion has tried to control and define mothering and—more importantly—how we can move past that. We'll explore what it means to mother as a source of strength, nourishment, and creativity, in a way that honors you just as much as the people, communities, or projects you're caring for.

Mary, the Good Mother

In patriarchal contexts, women's worth has historically been tied to their ability to bear children. From the earliest biblical stories, such as Sarah in the book of Genesis, women were often valued primarily for their role in producing heirs. Motherhood wasn't seen as a choice but as a duty to ensure lineage and societal survival. This rigid expectation came with little acknowledgment of a woman's autonomy or individual worth outside her ability to reproduce. Anything outside of this framework—choosing not to marry, infertility, or deciding not to have children—was labeled a deviation from the natural order. This reduction of a woman's identity to her reproductive role not only diminished her individuality but also stripped motherhood of the conscious, empowering choice it could be.

Perhaps no figure embodies this patriarchal ideal of motherhood more perfectly than Mary, the mother of Jesus. In Christian tradition, Mary is venerated as the ultimate "good mother": pure, obedient, and utterly devoted to her child. Her worth is directly tied to her ability to bear a son and her unwavering submission to God's will. She is celebrated for her willingness to accept the angel Gabriel's announcement without question, as seen in Luke 1:38, where she declares, "I am the Lord's servant. . . . May your word to me be fulfilled." This act of consent is framed not as a moment of agency but as a model of perfect obedience and submission.

Mary's portrayal in art and theology further reinforces this idealized image of the self-sacrificing mother. For instance, in *The Madonna of the Meadow* (1506) by Raphael, Mary is depicted seated in a serene landscape, tenderly cradling the infant Jesus and John the Baptist. Her expression is one of quiet devotion and humility, emphasizing her role as a nurturer and protector. The painting's idyllic beauty reinforces the narrative that Mary's identity is wholly tied to her role as a mother, with no hint of individuality beyond her caregiving. Similarly, in Michelangelo's *Pietà* (1498–1499), Mary cradles the crucified Jesus in her lap, her sorrow symbolizing ultimate selflessness and suffering for the sake of others. These depictions, while powerful, reduce Mary to an archetype of submission and sacrifice, sidelining any other dimension of her character. (You can see both at AngelaJHerrington.com/mother-mary.)

Mary's veneration as the ideal mother is further highlighted by the absence of her story beyond her relationship to Jesus. Her life outside the annunciation, pregnancy, birth, and death of Jesus remains largely untold. Apart from brief mentions in Acts, where she is present with the disciples, the New Testament gives little indication of her identity, desires, or contributions beyond motherhood. This absence underscores how her significance is tied almost entirely to her role as a mother, reinforcing the narrative that a woman's worth lies in her caregiving rather than in her individuality or autonomy.

Her image as the "perfect mother" reinforces the narrative that good mothering is not about choice but about duty, sacrifice, and erasure of the self. She is praised not for her own wisdom, dreams, or desires but for her ability to exist solely for the benefit of others.

The elevation of Mary as the archetypal "good mother" creates a template of motherhood that idealizes submission and selflessness while discouraging autonomy and personal fulfillment. She is celebrated for being a mother *who erases her own desires and identity to serve her child and God.* This ideal leaves little room for the complexities of real-life motherhood, where women often have to balance their needs, ambitions, and identities alongside their caregiving roles.

This reductionist view has far-reaching consequences, continuing to influence cultural attitudes about motherhood today. Women are still pressured to conform to an idealized version of motherhood that prioritizes the needs of others over their own, and to internalize the expectation that their ultimate purpose is to bear children. For many, this narrative stifles the creativity, joy, and nurturing power that motherhood could embody. By focusing solely on a woman's ability to sacrifice, patriarchal frameworks ignore the healing, creative, and empowering dimensions that mothering can encompass when approached as a conscious and autonomous choice.

It's worth noting that this framework of idealized, sacrificial motherhood is not universal. While this discussion focuses on Western history, many non-Western cultures offer alternative perspectives on motherhood, often valuing women's wisdom and contributions beyond reproduction. For example, in many Indigenous North American traditions, such as those of the Haudenosaunee Confederacy, mothers are deeply respected as leaders and caretakers of the community. Haudenosaunee women play critical roles in governance, holding decision-making power within their clans and ensuring the well-being of future generations. Andean Indigenous traditions in South America also honor mothers not only as nurturers of their families but also as stewards of Pachamama, or Mother

Earth, symbolizing a deep connection between nurturing life and sustaining the natural world.

These are just a few of the traditions that emphasize the holistic contributions of mothers, celebrating their leadership, healing abilities, and wisdom in guiding their communities. In contrast, the Western Christian patriarchal tradition has disproportionately linked motherhood with submission, leaving little room for women to embrace the fullness of their identities.

Motherhood, when reclaimed, has the potential to be more than duty and sacrifice. It can also be a path of healing, creativity, and connection, where the act of nurturing becomes reciprocal—feeding the mother's growth as much as her children's. By challenging the narrative that equates motherhood with submission, we can open up space for women to exist as whole, autonomous individuals who approach mothering as a conscious, nourishing choice that aligns with their values and desires.

Historical Context: How Did We Get Here?

In many ancient non-Christian societies, a wider view of motherhood was revered as sacred, with goddesses like Egypt's Isis and Greece's Gaia symbolizing fertility and protection. For instance, Isis was depicted nursing her infant son Horus, a scene that captured both her power as a creator and her role as a caretaker. These divine figures showed women's roles in creation and nurturing, though often tied to childbirth.

During medieval times, motherhood was seen as a woman's duty under the church's teachings, meant for producing heirs and managing the household, often without autonomy. For example, women were expected to uphold the ideal of "Marian virtues" such as humility and obedience, reflecting the image of the Virgin Mary as the model for all mothers. While women in Christian monastic life, like the abbess and mystic Hildegard of Bingen, embraced spiritual forms of motherhood, most were confined to roles of obedience.

The Renaissance brought some progress, especially for wealthy women who began to receive education. Figures like Christine de Pizan argued for the moral impact of educating women. Yet for most, motherhood remained tied to procreation, with societal value placed on raising children to continue family lines, rather than personal growth. These expectations were captured in art, such as Leonardo da Vinci's *Madonna of the Yarnwinder*, where Mary is pictured both as a loving mother and as symbolic of domestic diligence. (See AngelaJHerrington.com/mother-mary to view this painting.)

In the Enlightenment, motherhood became a woman's primary "natural state." Philosophers like Jean-Jacques Rousseau viewed a family founded on the mother's love as essential for raising moral citizens, reinforcing the belief that a woman's purpose was to nurture society through childrearing rather than self-development.[2] This era solidified the idea that women were inherently suited to caregiving roles, and their intellectual or creative ambitions were seen as detrimental to their "natural" duties.[3]

The Industrial Revolution entrenched domestic motherhood, with men as breadwinners and women as primary caregivers. As urbanization separated family roles (rather than the traditional rural model of men and women laboring alongside one another on the farm), women's contributions carried no obvious economic value, yet were essential. This created the ideal of the stay-at-home mother. The Victorian era further idealized this image, casting women as spiritual guides in the home but without personal agency and always under the headship of a male relative. In this era, publications like *Mrs. Beeton's Book of Household Management* instructed women on how to run their homes perfectly, presenting domesticity as a woman's noble duty.

The restrictive view of women's role in society continued into the twentieth century. Even the breaks in this pattern, such as when women entered the workforce out of necessity during

World War I and World War II, were usually met with an overcorrection when the men returned. Though women gained some workforce presence during wartime, societal expectations reset to domestic ideals. For example, advertising campaigns in the 1940s and 1950s, such as the "return to the kitchen" propaganda, encouraged women to leave their jobs and re-embrace traditional gender roles. Think about the stereotypical 1950s housewife; this hyperidealized domestic figure set the stage for the free love counterculture of the 1960s and 1970s. The backlash against free love was a catalyst for the rise of purity culture in the 1990s and early 2000s, which emphasized that a woman's primary role was to bear and raise children within a Christian, heterosexual marriage. Western culture continually reset to the idea of motherhood as duty rather than choice.

The Default Caregiver Inside and Outside the Home

The expectation that women are the default caregivers goes beyond raising children. While patriarchal systems view women's bodies primarily as vessels for creating life, they also cast women as emotional caretakers and domestic anchors, assuming that women's "natural" disposition makes them better suited for these roles. This expectation stretches far beyond just raising children; it includes managing the household, offering emotional labor, and providing care for others in the community, often without compensation or recognition.

The pressure to "do it all" persists in today's society. Women are expected to balance careers, maintain households, and raise children while managing their own emotions and those of their families. This type of mothering becomes a never-ending responsibility, with little space for the mother's own growth, rest, or self-care.

But where is the support for mothers? Too often, society assumes that caregiving is a woman's duty and fails to acknowledge the monumental labor that goes into raising children, maintaining homes, and nurturing communities. In contemporary culture, this expectation is often reinforced by media images of "super-moms," who seem to effortlessly balance work, childcare, and personal wellness—a fantasy that only adds to women's burden. When mothers ask for help, they are often met with judgment or told they are failing in their most basic duties. This is a deeply unfair expectation that perpetuates the cycles of self-sacrifice and burnout in women.

This expectation that women naturally serve as the default caregivers is a tool used by patriarchy to keep us separated from our own desires and dreams. It restricts our ability to say "No" to meeting other people's needs. By keeping women so busy with the emotional labor of caring for others, patriarchy ensures that we remain disconnected from our power, our creativity, and ultimately, from each other.

Yet, true mothering is not about depletion—it's about being filled with life-giving energy. Reclaiming this energy allows women to shift from "doing for others" to "nurturing with intention," making space for both caregiving and personal fulfillment. When we reclaim mothering as an act of nurturing and creating, rather than duty and obligation, we begin to see how vital it is to nurture ourselves in the process. This allows us to be present for those we care for without losing ourselves in the endless expectations of patriarchal caregiving.

Modern "Witches" Who Don't Embrace Patriarchal Motherhood

Mary's image as the perfect mother has long stood in contrast to the feared and vilified "witch" archetype—women whose wisdom, independence, and power threatened the status quo. Where Mary is praised for her obedience and self-sacrifice, the old witch in the woods represents the woman who refuses to shrink, who owns her wisdom and power unapologetically.

The old witch in the woods archetype represents only one face of the "dangerous woman" in patriarchal mythology. The wicked stepmother, suffragettes who demanded equality, feminists who insist that basic rights apply to women too, and modern politicians and activists who fight for women's bodily autonomy—all have been labeled as witches. This label isn't just historical; it persists in modern political rhetoric, where women who assert their rights are called "nasty" or "radical." These women are portrayed as threats to the social order and Christian values simply because they challenge the norms of womanhood and motherhood.

The wicked stepmother in fairy tales stands as a warning against what happens when we reject the "good mother" ideal. Unlike Mary, who is self-sacrificial and nurturing, the wicked stepmother is depicted as jealous, manipulative, and selfish—traits that clash with the expectation that a woman should always place others' needs before her own. Like the biblical Jezebel, she is power-hungry and brutal. Her desire to assert her own will, rather than dissolve into selflessness, casts her as a villain, illustrating the cultural anxiety surrounding women who prioritize themselves or disrupt the family hierarchy.

Understanding these archetypes allows us to question who benefits from these labels and to recognize the power of women who refuse to conform. Reclaiming autonomy and wisdom from these cultural myths liberates women to embody their fullest potential without fear of judgment or reprisal.

Mothering Beyond Patriarchal Definitions

Mothering, in its truest form, is about so much more than just birthing or raising babies. It's about nurturing, creating, and holding space for others and yourself. Whether or not you've physically given birth, you have the power to mother in ways that bring life, healing, and compassion to everything you touch—whether that's caring for your community, nurturing your creativity, or offering emotional support to those around you. You don't have to be a mother in the traditional sense to embody the energy of mothering.

When we step outside the narrow definitions of motherhood imposed by patriarchal systems, we reclaim mothering as an act of empowerment and creativity. Mothering becomes a way to heal and nourish both ourselves and those around us, without the expectation that we must sacrifice our own well-being in the process. The archetypal mother is a force of emotional support, wisdom, and creation that transcends biological ties. She nurtures life in countless ways—through art, activism, or simply holding space for others. This kind of mothering isn't a duty or societal expectation but a conscious choice that women make because it brings them fulfillment, not because it's demanded of them.

But rejecting patriarchal definitions of motherhood doesn't automatically erase the very real challenges that mothers and caregivers face, especially in societies that lack robust social safety nets. In many places, women still shoulder the majority of caregiving responsibilities while also navigating work, relationships, and personal growth. For some, the expectation to "do it all" leaves little space for honoring their own needs, even when they actively resist patriarchal ideals. Recognizing these constraints is essential if we're to have an honest conversation about reclaiming mothering as a source of empowerment.

When we embrace a soulful mothering, there's still room to acknowledge the structural challenges that make it difficult to prioritize ourselves. It's not about pretending we always have time, energy, or resources in abundance, but about holding space for the belief that we *deserve* to nurture our own needs alongside those we care for. This isn't an act of indulgence—it's an act of survival and restoration in a system that often overlooks the caregivers who keep communities and families afloat. Soulful mothering is about recognizing our worth and refusing to let the absence of external support erode the love and care we give ourselves.

We mother ourselves not because others depend on us but because we are worthy of the same love, compassion, and attention we give to others. This kind of mothering is rooted in personal choice, allowing women to reclaim their power and autonomy while creating life—whether literal, emotional, or creative—in ways that matter most to them.

Soulful mothering also involves advocating for systemic change. It's not just about individual empowerment but about imagining and building communities where no one is left to carry the load alone. This collective approach to caregiving ensures that mothering remains a life-giving act, not one that drains us of our own vitality. It acknowledges the reality of our current systems while making space for the hope that together we can create something better.

Mothering Beyond the "Sinful, Broken" Woman Trope

The sinful, broken woman trope—which tells us we must outwork our brokenness and constantly atone for Eve's sin—has confined women to roles of submission and self-sacrifice for far too long. This trope robs us of our own wisdom, creativity, and autonomy by framing motherhood as an obligation rather than an empowered choice. It's a slightly modified version of the old witch in the woods mythology: Both tropes shame and fear women for their power, autonomy, and wisdom. When we reject this narrative, we call the witch out of the woods, reclaiming our ability to mother ourselves and others with strength, creativity, and intuition.

We see this trope play out in cultural expectations that label women who are childless by choice as "selfish" or incomplete. For example, public discourse often scrutinizes high-profile women like Oprah Winfrey or Dolly Parton for not having children, implying that their remarkable achievements aren't enough because they haven't fulfilled the patriarchal expectation of motherhood. This persistent narrative suggests that women's worth is tied to their ability to nurture others, rather than their own autonomy, passions, or contributions to society. It positions women as inherently incomplete unless they are sacrificing for someone else, perpetuating the belief that we must atone for our so-called brokenness through caregiving.

When we reject this narrative, we step into a more expansive, nourishing version of mothering—one that honors the wisdom we carry within us, celebrates our creativity, and allows us to flourish in all areas of life. True mothering isn't about martyrdom—it's about flourishing. When we reframe mothering as an act of life-giving energy, we open ourselves up to new possibilities for connection, creativity, and joy. Mothering becomes a way to create life, nurture relationships, and honor our own wisdom, without the constraints of patriarchal ideals.

Mothering, then, becomes a creative, life-giving force that extends far beyond the family unit. It's about nurturing life in all its forms, whether through art, culture, or community-building. For example, activists like Harriet Tubman and Dolores Huerta embodied mothering as they nurtured movements for justice, freedom, and equity. Tubman's efforts to guide enslaved people to freedom through the Underground Railroad and Huerta's tireless advocacy for farm workers demonstrate how mothering can extend far beyond biology. These women nurtured entire communities, fostering growth, resilience, and liberation.

When we expand our understanding of what it means to mother, we move beyond the narrow definitions imposed by patriarchal systems. Women are free to mother in ways that resonate with them, whether through activism, mentorship, or simply showing up for those they love. Motherhood becomes a celebration of creativity, nourishment, and compassion—a way of giving life to what matters most.

Ultimately, motherhood outside the conservative Christian patriarchy is about trusting choice, empowerment, and creativity. It's about each of us embracing our inner mother without the pressure to conform to traditional roles or expectations. This view honors the woman as much as the care she provides, allowing her to thrive alongside those she nurtures.

Mothering can be a conscious, empowered choice, where our needs and desires are just as valued as those of the people, projects, and communities we nurture. By reclaiming our true power as nurturers, creators, and healers, we can rewrite the story of mothering. We no longer have to fit into the box of the "good mother" who sacrifices herself for others. Instead, we can choose to mother in ways that nurture us and those we care for, allowing us to thrive as whole, complex beings.

Mothering, especially learning to mother ourselves, becomes a sacred act of liberation that changes everything. At its most expansive, it's about learning to hold space for ourselves as we would for someone we love. For many of us, however, this requires filling gaps left by the nurturing, teaching, and support we didn't receive growing up. Whether those who raised us were unable or unwilling to provide that foundation, self-mothering allows us to reconnect with the parts of ourselves that still yearn for acceptance, encouragement, and care. This is not only a path toward reclaiming our fullest selves but also a means of breaking generational patterns of lack, trauma, and disconnection.

Mothering Ourselves

Self-mothering involves recognizing where we feel unseen, unloved, or unable to trust ourselves—and choosing to step in as our own source of nurturing and support. Through this process, we learn to shift from seeking validation externally to finding it within ourselves. Where we once looked to others for approval or self-worth, self-mothering guides us to recognize that our worth is inherent, not dependent on others' opinions or responses. This internal validation strengthens our sense of self, helping us build confidence in who we are apart from the approval of others. It allows us to cultivate self-trust, where we validate our experiences, needs, and feelings rather than relying on someone else to do it for us.

As we learn to nurture and love ourselves, self-mothering also helps us shift from attachment to others to a stable, loving attachment with ourselves. Rather than looking for fulfillment in others, we develop a deeper, lasting connection with ourselves—a grounding that enables us to feel whole and worthy on our own. This self-attachment creates an inner stability that allows us to form healthier, more balanced relationships with others, free from neediness or codependence. We become our own source of security, able to meet our needs and offer compassion to ourselves in ways we may have longed for but never received.

For many of us, the journey of self-mothering begins by creating a sense of safety and belonging. This involves establishing routines, practices, or spaces that make us feel grounded and at home within ourselves. By creating these stable internal foundations, we can begin to trust ourselves more deeply, make decisions aligned with our true desires, and feel rooted and calm amidst life's inevitable uncertainties.

Reparenting through compassion is an essential part of self-mothering, allowing us to approach our inner selves with understanding rather than criticism. We can start by visualizing the younger versions of ourselves—the child within who longed for love, acceptance, or guidance—and extending compassion toward that part of ourselves. Offering this kindness to ourselves rewrites the narrative of worth that we may have grown up with, helping us to see ourselves as deserving of love and care, no matter what.

Nurturing our inner child is also a vital piece of the process, allowing us to fill unmet needs and create a sense of inner wholeness. The wounded parts of ourselves are often connected to childhood experiences where we felt abandoned, unseen, or pressured to meet impossible standards. Self-mothering invites us to embrace those parts of ourselves by allowing them space to express play, rest, or curiosity without pressure or fear. This nurturing approach not only fills unmet needs but also allows us to experience joy, creativity, and freedom, strengthening our relationship with ourselves.

Through self-mothering, we shift the need for validation from others to the self, building an internal foundation of self-respect, acceptance, and love. This internalization of love and worth allows us to release harmful narratives and begin to trust the truth of our inherent worth. The more we connect with ourselves in this compassionate, nurturing way, the more fully we can rewrite generational patterns of scarcity, trauma, and emotional neglect, creating a legacy of wholeness and inner abundance that transforms the future.

Leaning In: Mothering Your Younger Self

In this activity, you'll connect with the archetypal mother within yourself to nurture a tender part of you that needs love and care. This practice will guide you toward self-mothering in a way that feels restorative and deeply personal, helping you create a safe, healing space for yourself.

Step 1: Find a Safe and Nurturing Space

Choose a quiet and comfortable place where you won't be disturbed. Light a candle, play soft music, or bring in objects that make you feel grounded and safe. This space should feel like a sanctuary—a place where you can be fully present with yourself.

Step 2: Connect with Your Younger Self

Close your eyes and take a few deep breaths. Allow yourself to picture a younger version of you in a moment in time that feels tender or is calling to be explored. Visualize this younger self sitting with you. What do they look like? What emotions do they carry? What is drawing your attention to this moment?

Step 3: Get Down on Their Level

Imagine yourself physically and emotionally meeting your younger self at their level. Sit with them, observe their body language, and gently ask, "What hurts?" Create space for their response, whether it comes as words, emotions, or images.

Step 4: Speak the Words You Needed

Let your response flow from your heart. Speak the words to your younger self that you needed to hear in that moment. Offer reassurance, love, and compassion. Let your emotions flow freely without judgment—this is your time to offer the care and support you needed but may not have received.

Step 5: Reflect and Journal

When the moment feels complete, sit with your younger self for as long as they need. When you're ready, pick up your journal and jot down notes about your conversation. Reflect on what was shared, the emotions that arose, and how your body felt before, during, and after the activity. Be gentle with yourself as you process these reflections.

CHAPTER 4

Nourishing Self

Patriarchal systems have long equated a woman's worth with her capacity for self-sacrifice. We are taught that our value is tied to how much we can give to our families, communities, and others, often leaving little room for ourselves. This system glorifies the idea that a "good woman" puts everyone else first, and this expectation becomes a powerful force in shaping how we see ourselves. We're led to believe that if we aren't tirelessly serving others, we're somehow falling short of what it means to be a worthy, valuable woman.

One of the most damaging aspects of this conditioning is the belief that endless giving is synonymous with holiness. Biblical narratives, like Proverbs 31, often depict the "ideal" woman as someone who tirelessly serves her family and community. This image reinforces the expectation that our worth comes from how much we can sacrifice, making it difficult to set boundaries or take time for ourselves without feeling guilty or selfish.

This toxic cycle also thrives on the idea that we must enable dependency by doing everything for others. We are praised for taking on the emotional and physical labor of caregiving without question, and keeping things running smoothly—whether at home, in the community, or in religious spaces. However, this form of "selflessness" traps us in cycles of overwork and emotional exhaustion, leaving little room for our own needs. Patriarchal systems benefit from this because when we're busy and exhausted, we remain stuck in survival mode, unable to catch our breath long enough to challenge the structures that keep us there.

Much of the labor we perform is unpaid, invisible, and unrecognized. Whether caring for children (our own or someone else's), maintaining the household, or organizing community or religious events, our contributions are often taken for granted—seen as just part of what it means to be a woman. This labor is considered "natural" for us, leaving us with little time, energy, and resources to pursue our passions or to rest.

The consequences of this invisible labor are profound. It leads to burnout—emotionally, mentally, physically, and spiritually. We're left depleted, with little room for creativity, joy, or personal growth. Living in survival mode becomes the norm, as we constantly give without receiving rest or support. This cycle drains our sense of self-worth and keeps us disconnected from our own needs and desires, reinforcing the belief that our value is only in what we can provide to others.

Generational Patterns of Exploitation

The expectation of self-sacrifice is passed down through generations, creating cycles of self-neglect that are often disguised as virtues like holiness, strength, resilience, or duty. Women model this behavior for their daughters, who grow up believing their worth is tied to their ability to sacrifice endlessly, too. These patterns are further reinforced by societal myths like the American "bootstrapping" ideal—the belief that anyone can succeed and flourish if they work hard enough.

The idea that anyone can "pull themselves up by their bootstraps" and achieve success if they work hard enough plays into our struggle to resist exploitation. While this narrative may inspire individualism and perseverance for those in power, it also places the blame for unmet needs squarely on the shoulders of those who struggle. Women, particularly those in working-class and middle-class families, are told that if they are not thriving, it is because they are not working hard enough, sacrificing enough, or pushing themselves to the limit.

However, this myth fails to acknowledge that many women are often trapped in systems that actively prevent them from flourishing. The promise of equal opportunity is flawed because it overlooks the historical and structural barriers that disproportionately affect marginalized groups. Generations of women—especially those from communities impacted by legacies of enslavement, genocide, forced immigration, and systemic racism—have inherited a culture of scarcity that teaches us to put our own needs last.

Now, more than ever, the playing field is far from level. Not everyone starts with the same opportunities or resources, and the burden of caregiving and unpaid labor disproportionately falls on women. Women get caught in cycles of exhaustion, constantly being told that they should be able to do it all without complaint or compensation.

Rest, Exploitation, and Generational Trauma

The intersectionality of generational trauma and exploitation further complicates the idea that we all deserve rest and nourishment. Communities impacted by the legacies of enslavement, genocide, and forced migration due to conflict or persecution (such as refugees and immigrants) often inherit the material scars of these histories and a cultural mindset of scarcity. The narrative passed down in these communities is one of survival, not flourishing. Women in these communities are often taught that their needs are secondary to the survival of the family or the community as a whole.

For African American women whose ancestors endured centuries of enslavement, the expectation of self-sacrifice is deeply embedded. During the two-and-a-half centuries of American slavery, Black women were forced to labor for others while their own families were torn apart. Many were sexually assaulted and exploited by abusive enslavers, sometimes repeatedly being forced to bear their children. Even after emancipation, systemic racism continued to deny Black women opportunities for rest, compensation, and autonomy. While Black men faced similar racial oppression, women faced additional and complex layers of gender bias, even within their own communities. The pressure on Black women to carry their community increased as Black men were targeted by racism, hate crimes, and a deeply racist justice system.[1]

The same pattern extends to Indigenous women, whose ancestors faced genocide, forced assimilation, and the erasure of their cultural and spiritual practices. For immigrant and refugee women today, the expectation of self-sacrifice often comes in the form of working multiple jobs in addition to caring for families, all in the hope of providing a better life for the next generation.

The Colonial Legacy: Stripping Away Resources and People

For many of us, the lingering effects of colonialism play a significant role in our experiences of scarcity and exploitation. Colonialism wasn't just about political dominance—it was a structured system designed to strip away resources and people from colonized regions to increase the wealth and flourishing of the few while decimating the populations and lands under colonization. The colonizers thrived on the backs of those whose lands, labor, and bodies were taken from them.

This violent legacy remains alive today. Many of us, especially those from historically colonized regions or marginalized communities, are still living on the edge of poverty—not just financially, but emotionally, spiritually, and mentally. We exist in a heightened state of alert, constantly worrying that what we have and what we do is not enough. Colonialism left behind a mindset of scarcity and fear, ensuring that entire populations, particularly women, would be kept in survival mode. The resources—whether land, wealth, or emotional capacity—were taken, and the colonized were left with little but the burden of rebuilding under oppressive structures.

For women whose ancestors endured chattel slavery, genocide, gender-based violence, or displacement, the legacy of those traumas lives on, not just in cultural memory but in the very fabric of their being. This inherited trauma contributes to the cycles of burnout, depletion, and survival mode that many women experience today.

Even when we believe we have moved on from past wounds, our bodies may carry the legacy of that suffering, influencing how we respond to the world and limiting our capacity to flourish.

Breaking Free from the Theology of Punishment

The story of Eve has been used as a powerful tool to control and suppress women for generations, reinforcing the belief that women must atone for the original sin through their pain, suffering, and sacrifice. Eve was blamed for humanity's fall from grace because she took the first bite of the forbidden fruit in Genesis 3, which canonized the idea that women were inherently weaker, more prone to sin, and in need of male guidance. Kimberly A. Hamlin, author of the 2014 book *From Eve to Evolution: Darwin, Science, and Women's Rights in Gilded Age America*, stated that one "can not overestimate how important Adam and Eve were in terms of constraining and shaping people's ideas about women."[2] Christian patriarchal systems have long taught that women's worth is tied to their ability to serve others, endure hardship, and accept their role as subservient caregivers. This theology frames women's suffering as holy and just, making us feel that our needs must always come second to those of our families, communities, or male counterparts.

Christian teachings often argue that women are inherently flawed, that our desires and instincts are dangerous, and that the only way to redeem ourselves from Eve's mistake is through endless self-sacrifice. Women are conditioned to view their own pain as a necessary burden, reinforcing the belief that personal boundaries and self-care are acts of selfishness rather than essential parts of flourishing. Just as the old witch in the woods has been feared and vilified for not carrying the burdens of the community, patriarchy has used the story of Eve to convince women that their instincts, desires, and autonomy are selfish, lead to immense pain, and harm others. This doctrine of punishment keeps women in cycles of burnout, guilt, and self-neglect, never allowing us to fully embrace our own worth.

But there is a way out. Setting boundaries and prioritizing self-care is an act of resistance against this theology. When women begin to challenge these teachings, we start to understand that flourishing—physically, emotionally, and spiritually—is not something we must earn through suffering. Instead, it is our birthright. Reclaiming space for ourselves allows women to see that our inherent value does not depend on how much we give to others or how well we endure hardship.

By rejecting the idea that suffering is necessary for redemption, women step into their power and autonomy. We begin to challenge the systems that have exploited women for centuries and reclaim the parts of ourselves that have been buried under layers of guilt and shame. We learn to trust our own instincts and desires, realizing that caring for ourselves is not an act of rebellion that deserves to be punished, but one of healing and self-compassion.

It's Time to Reject the "Making Up for Eve" Narrative

At the core of this harmful theology is the story of Eve, which has long been used to justify keeping women small, mistrusting ourselves, and dependent on male authority. The narrative frames Eve as the ultimate betrayer of goodness and holiness, suggesting that women, by nature, are weak, easily deceived, and prone to failure. This story teaches women that we cannot trust ourselves, our instincts, or our wisdom, reinforcing a sense of internalized self-doubt.

By continually pointing to Eve's sin as the root of human suffering, Christian patriarchy creates a powerful narrative that diminishes women's confidence and strength. The message is clear: Women are prone to error, and their wisdom must be questioned. This undermines not only a woman's relationship with herself but also her connections with other women. Eve's story fosters mistrust among women, making it difficult to rely on each other or share the kind of communal wisdom that might empower us.

Rejecting this narrative means reclaiming trust in ourselves and our feminine wisdom. It's about acknowledging that our strength, intuition, and insight are powerful, not flawed. It's about breaking free from the idea that we are inherently deceivers or betrayers. This shift allows women to reconnect with ourselves and each other in profound ways, rebuilding bonds of trust and solidarity that patriarchal systems have long sought to sever.

As we reject the Eve narrative, we also reject the limitations it places on our lives. We are no longer confined to roles of endless sacrifice, submission, and suffering. Instead, we can explore our full potential, embrace joy, and live in alignment with our true desires and passions. The power of rejecting this harmful narrative lies in its ability to open up a world where women are no longer held back by fear, guilt, or shame. Instead, we are free to flourish, create, and live fully, knowing that we are worthy of love, care, and fulfillment—not because we have earned it through suffering, but because every human inherently deserves it.

The Cost of Neglecting Our Own Needs

Many women have been conditioned to ignore the profound damage caused by neglecting our own needs. This learned behavior, taught and reinforced through generations, isn't simply a personal flaw or failure; it's rooted in a much deeper, systemic issue. The church's toxic teachings about feminine wisdom and experience being inherently sinful or weak have left women feeling disconnected from our power, worth, and ability to flourish.

When women internalize the belief that our value is determined by how much we serve others, we lose sight of our personal needs. We are taught that prioritizing self-care is selfish, reinforcing a cycle of guilt, shame, and self-loathing. Boundaries—so essential to flourishing—become taboo, as they threaten the system built on women's constant over-giving and self-sacrifice.

The impact of this self-neglect goes far beyond simple tiredness or frustration. It cuts to the core of a woman's sense of self, eroding her confidence, her self-worth, and her sense of purpose. The burnout that follows is not just physical; it is spiritual, emotional, and mental. Women who have been taught that our worth lies in how much we give often feel spiritually depleted, as though we've lost our connection to the Divine and to our inner self. The constant demands placed upon us leave little room for reflection, spiritual growth, or personal well-being.

This chronic overwork and neglect of self also takes a toll on women's health. Under the pressure of caregiving and the endless expectations of service, women's bodies begin to break down. Chronic stress, illness, and fatigue become common experiences, but they are too often normalized as part of a woman's "duty."

The emotional consequences are devastating. Women become disconnected from ourselves and our desires, making it difficult to form healthy, equitable, meaningful relationships with others. The exhaustion from overwork leaves little emotional energy to invest in deep connections with friends, partners, or even our own children. We live in a constant state of depletion, unable to give the best of ourselves to anyone because we've been giving everything for too long.

Perhaps most destructive is the way this cycle of neglect keeps women in survival mode. The fight-or-flight response becomes a constant state, as women live in high-stress environments without the resources—time, space, rest—to break free. This state of constant alertness wrecks our bodies, stifles creativity, limits emotional growth, and prevents women from imagining a life beyond the grind of daily demands. The weight of expectations keeps us trapped, unable to dream, to grow, or to create the life we deserve.

The result is a cycle of limitation, a life lived in the shadow of what could be, all because women have been taught that our needs are less important, less worthy, and even dangerous. This is the toxic legacy of the church's teaching that women's wisdom and desires are sinful or weak. By encouraging women to see themselves as vessels of service—rather than as whole, complex beings with our own needs—the church and patriarchy have created generations of women who believe that flourishing is something they don't deserve.

But the truth is that this belief system is designed to keep women small. It's designed to keep women from stepping into our power, creativity, and divine right to flourish in every area of life. This moment can be the turning point—the moment where we can choose to break free from the lies we've been told and reclaim our birthright to thrive. It is time to recognize the cost of neglecting ourselves and to understand that we are not here to merely survive. We are here to flourish.

How Burnout and Overwork Prevent Flourishing

Burnout goes far beyond physical exhaustion; it seeps into every corner of our lives, draining our emotional, mental, and creative energy. The constant cycle of giving without receiving, of pouring from an empty cup, leaves little room for joy, inspiration, or personal growth. Over time, this depletion erodes our ability to dream, plan, or create the kind of life that brings true fulfillment.

When we are locked in caregiving roles, the demands placed on us begin to take a toll on our spiritual health as well. The endless to-do lists and responsibilities leave little space for personal reflection or a deeper connection with the Divine. Instead of flourishing spiritually, we find ourselves feeling disconnected, spiritually exhausted, and distant from the practices or beliefs that once nourished us.

As the burnout continues, it doesn't just impact our emotional or spiritual well-being; our physical health is also threatened. Chronic stress builds up in our bodies, leading to fatigue, illness, and other symptoms that reinforce the cycle of depletion. We become so focused on caring for others that we neglect our own well-being, believing that our health is somehow less important. This physical toll only deepens the exhaustion, making it even harder to break free from the burnout cycle.

One of the most painful effects of burnout is how it affects our relationships. When we are emotionally depleted, it becomes difficult to form meaningful connections with others. The energy needed to nurture intimacy, whether with friends, partners, or even our children, simply isn't there. We might find ourselves retreating or feeling detached, as the exhaustion makes it nearly impossible to sustain the deep emotional connections that once mattered to us.

The root of this burnout lies in more than just overwork; it's the result of a belief system that tells us we are only valuable when we are sacrificing for others. This belief—one deeply ingrained in patriarchal culture—tells us that self-care is selfish and that our worth comes from how much we can endure. We are taught that suffering is a necessary part of atoning for Eve's original sin, leaving us to believe that endless labor and sacrifice are somehow righteous. This keeps us trapped in survival mode, unable to experience the joy, fulfillment, or growth that flourishing requires.

Patriarchy keeps women in a constant state of burnout and overwork because it knows that when we are disconnected from our own energy and creativity, we are less likely to challenge the systems that keep us small. When we are stuck in this survival mode, or burdened by the chronic stress of overwork, our cognitive and emotional resources are depleted, making it harder to step outside the system's expectations or challenge the limiting beliefs that keep us small. We can't flourish or work for change when we're always on high alert, focused solely on getting through the day.

Burnout leaves us disconnected from our power, our spirituality, and our relationships. It keeps us running on empty, unable to dream of a better way, and trapped in a cycle that limits our capacity to experience the fullness of life. To break free from this cycle, we must first recognize that caring for ourselves is not a selfish act—it is a necessary step toward reclaiming our energy, our joy, and our ability to thrive.

What's Possible: Rewriting the Narrative of Self-Care and Flourishing

When we begin to challenge and reject these narratives of self-sacrifice and scarcity, we open up the possibility for a new way of living—one where women prioritize their own flourishing and well-being, not just survival. By recognizing and acknowledging the systems that have kept us small and the generational traumas that have been passed down, we create space for healing, joy, and growth.

When we challenge and reject the toxic narratives that tell us we are only worthy when we give endlessly, we create space to rewrite our stories. The truth is, when we meet our own needs and prioritize flourishing, a whole new world of possibilities opens up, including:

- *Greater capacity for joy and fulfillment*
  When women set healthy boundaries and prioritize our own well-being, we reclaim the time and energy needed to pursue what truly brings us joy. Instead of constantly pouring from an empty cup, we can focus on activities, relationships, and passions that nourish us deeply.
- *Stronger, healthier relationships*
  Relationships no longer have to be rooted in codependency or obligation. With boundaries in place, we are free to engage in healthier, more balanced relationships where we are valued for who we are, not just what we can give. Our relationships are built on mutual respect, trust, and emotional connection, allowing both parties to flourish.
- *Room for creativity, growth, and purpose*
  When women are no longer drained by the expectations of overwork and endless caregiving, we have the freedom to dream, create, and contribute in meaningful ways. Whether through art, career pursuits, activism, or simply reclaiming hobbies and personal interests, flourishing allows women to embrace our creative potential and contribute to the world from a place of wholeness.
- *Spiritual renewal and connection*
  By breaking free from the narrative that self-sacrifice is the only path to righteousness, women can reconnect with our spirituality on our own terms. Flourishing creates the space for deeper spiritual reflection,

divine connection, and personal growth that nourishes our souls and revitalizes faith.

- *A life rooted in purpose, not obligation*
  When women reject the idea that our value is tied to our ability to serve others, we reclaim the ability to define our lives on our own terms. Flourishing isn't about survival—it's about living a life that is aligned with our true purpose, passions, and desires. It's about thriving in every sense: emotionally, spiritually, creatively, and physically.

When we learn to reject exploitation and prioritize flourishing, we can reclaim our time, energy, and many aspects of our health while modeling this behavior for the next generation. Flourishing should not be a privilege reserved for the few; it is the birthright of all women. But we must also recognize that the ability to flourish is not equally accessible to everyone. Systemic inequities—rooted in racism, ableism, economic disparity, and other forms of oppression—continue to strip many women of the resources and opportunities needed to prioritize their well-being. These injustices disproportionately affect women of color, women with disabilities, and those living in poverty, making the pursuit of flourishing feel out of reach for many.

Reclaiming flourishing is a revolutionary act precisely because it pushes back against the systems that have kept so many women marginalized. It requires us not only to reject personal exploitation but also to confront the larger structures of injustice that perpetuate inequality. True flourishing must go beyond individual acts of self-care; it must include collective action that dismantles the barriers preventing women from accessing the physical, emotional, financial, and spiritual resources they need to thrive.

For those of us who hold privilege in this unjust system, part of our healing journey involves learning to leverage our resources—time, money, support networks, or access to power—not just for ourselves, but to create space for those who don't have the same opportunities. This isn't about white saviorism or imposing solutions that reinforce existing hierarchies. Instead, it's about fostering autonomy, listening to the needs of marginalized communities, and supporting their self-defined paths to healing and development. True support means resisting the urge to pressure or shape others to "fit in" to our culture and instead creating systems and spaces that honor diverse experiences and paths to flourishing.

We must also hold space for the complexity of this work. For some, flourishing may feel like a distant goal when survival itself is a daily challenge. Reclaiming our birthright to thrive does not mean ignoring or minimizing the very real struggles many women face. Instead, it means acknowledging those struggles and working to create a world where flourishing becomes possible for all—not just as an ideal, but as a tangible reality. By addressing these systemic inequities, we honor the collective strength of women while ensuring that no one is left behind on the path toward flourishing.

This reclamation is not just about self-empowerment; it's about solidarity and a shared commitment to creating a world where every woman can live fully, freely, and without fear. By prioritizing flourishing as an act of resistance, we reject the narrative that women's worth is tied to self-sacrifice and scarcity. Instead, we embrace a vision of abundance, healing, and liberation that honors the interconnectedness of all women and their unique paths toward thriving.

Begin with Reclaiming Space for Flourishing

We've been conditioned to believe that focusing on our own needs is selfish, but the reality is that reclaiming space for ourselves is essential to our well-being. By giving ourselves moments of rest and reflection, we allow our minds and bodies to reset. Taking time to be present with ourselves, even in small ways, can have a profound impact on how we show up in the world.

For example, simply enjoying your morning coffee without distractions might seem insignificant, but it can be a powerful act of mindfulness. This small moment of stillness helps you start the day from a place of calm rather than rushing into the demands of others. Saying "no" when you feel overextended can also change the way you view your own worth. It teaches you that your energy is valuable, and it reminds others to respect your limits, ultimately freeing you to feel more at peace.

When we continually pour ourselves into others without taking time to refill our own cup, we miss out on opportunities to grow, create, and flourish. Shifting even a little of your energy back toward yourself can open doors to greater joy, inspiration, and personal fulfillment. This is not about abandoning your responsibilities but about honoring yourself alongside them.

If you've always wanted to explore a hobby or creative pursuit, taking that first step, no matter how small, is incredibly affirming. It reminds you that your passions matter and that you deserve to enjoy them. This can reignite a sense of curiosity and excitement about life, helping you break free from the mundane cycle of giving without receiving. Taking short, intentional breaks throughout your day—whether it's stretching, going for a walk, or simply breathing—can help you reconnect with yourself, reducing stress and boosting your mood. These small changes in focus can shift your energy toward something that replenishes you.

Designating a small part of your day or week to do something that nurtures you—like a creative hobby, a quiet meditation, or time spent in nature—can profoundly affect your mental and emotional state. When you invest in yourself, you show others that your well-being is just as important as anyone else's. This replenished energy will naturally spill over into how you care for others, allowing you to give from a place of abundance rather than depletion. Even creating a small, calming space in your home, whether it's a cozy reading nook or a corner for quiet reflection, can remind you daily that your needs deserve to be met.

By giving yourself permission to rest without guilt—whether it's taking a nap or an evening to relax—you are affirming that your worth is not tied to how much you accomplish or give. This shift in mindset can lead to deeper physical, emotional, and spiritual healing. Likewise, creating a personal ritual, such as lighting a candle and reflecting on what brings you joy before bed, can transform your daily routine into an intentional practice of self-care. These simple acts build a life that nourishes you from within, allowing you to flourish with energy, joy, and purpose.

Flourishing requires more than just pushing through each day; it demands that we create the space and energy needed for rest, nourishment, growth, joy, and fulfillment. When we make even small adjustments to prioritize our needs, the effects are transformative. Reclaiming our energy doesn't mean we stop caring for others; it means we care for ourselves in ways that allow us to show up more fully in all areas of life.

Leaning In: Discovering What Is Missing

Identifying something that seems to be missing is a great place to start nourishing yourself. I'd encourage you to hone in on something that might seem selfish, childish, or unproductive to explore it with curiosity and wonder. The goal is not necessarily to achieve it immediately, but to reconnect with the part of yourself that desires it and to begin nurturing that desire in meaningful ways.

Step 1: Reflect on What Feels Missing

Take a moment to sit quietly with your thoughts. Ask yourself:

- What is one thing I've always wanted to do but haven't because it felt "selfish" or impractical?

- What makes me feel alive, joyful, or at ease?
- Is there something I've been putting off because it feels too indulgent or out of reach?

Write down whatever comes to mind, even if it feels small or silly. This is about being honest with yourself and recognizing what you long for.

Step 2: Choose One Thing to Focus On

From your reflections, pick one thing to focus on this week. It could be something playful, relaxing, or adventurous—whatever feels like it would bring you joy or fulfillment. For example:

- Treating yourself to an afternoon off for rest or creativity.
- Planning a solo mini-vacation or even just a morning at a café with no agenda.
- Reclaiming a childhood hobby like painting, playing an instrument, or baking.

Step 3: Engage with the Idea Curiously

If your chosen activity isn't something you can immediately do, explore ways to engage with it this week in small, manageable steps. For example:

- If it's a solo trip, start thinking about where you might go, when it could fit into your calendar, and what you'd need to make it happen.
- If it's a creative activity, gather your materials or spend time browsing for inspiration.
- If it's rest, plan a day where you can schedule less and focus on being present with yourself.
- Be careful not to let the planning process become overwhelming or a chore. Keep your focus on curiosity and excitement, rather than perfection.

Step 4: Notice How It Feels

Throughout the week, take note of how this activity—or even the idea of it—makes you feel. Does it spark joy, ease, or a sense of wonder? Are there feelings of resistance or guilt that arise? Write these observations in your journal to better understand how you relate to and experience self-nourishment.

Step 5: Commit to One Small Action

Before the week is over, take one concrete step toward experiencing this missing piece in your life. Whether it's setting a date for your mini-vacation, carving out time to rest, or spending an hour on your chosen activity, honor your commitment to yourself.

Step 6: Reflect and Celebrate

At the end of the week, revisit your journal and reflect on the experience. Did this process help you reconnect with yourself? What did you learn about your desires, and how can you continue to nurture them? Celebrate the steps you've taken, no matter how small, and remind yourself that caring for your own needs is a valuable act of self-love.

Chapter 5

Pleasure

Come As You Are author Emily Nagoski describes pleasure as a measure of well-being, not something we measure by the frequency or other quantitative data.[1] Let that sink in for a moment. Pleasure—something that feels so natural, so innate—has the power to guide us toward what nourishes and sustains us. And yet, for so many of us raised in Christian patriarchal systems, this wisdom of the body has been ignored, twisted, or outright denied.

We're often taught that pleasure is dangerous, especially for women. Feminine sensuality and erotic pleasure for its own sake are labeled as sinful, selfish, or even deviant. In conservative and fundamentalist communities, pleasure is divided into two rigid categories: the kind shared with others (and sanctioned by God) and the kind experienced solely for oneself. The first is holy, while the second—particularly when tied to sexuality or sensuality—is seen as a distortion of God's gifts.

What's rarely discussed is how this framework of "acceptable pleasure" is designed to control women. The pleasure that serves others—whether through procreation, pleasing a spouse, or fulfilling societal expectations—is upheld as virtuous. But the pleasure that serves you? That's framed as indulgent or even dangerous. This system reduces women to tools, valuable only for what we can provide. It teaches us to distrust our inner knowing, to question what feels good, and to believe our bodies are not truly ours.

Think about the implications of this. If your pleasure is only valid when it benefits someone else, where does that leave you? These narratives keep us disconnected from our own bodies, our desires, and the deep satisfaction that comes from experiencing pleasure purely for ourselves. They tell us that our bodies exist not for our own joy but as commodities to be managed, controlled, and given away.

Before we can reimagine pleasure in a way that's expansive and life-affirming, we need to confront the root of this disconnection: the fear of women's erotic pleasure. For centuries, patriarchal systems have worked to frame sexual pleasure for its own sake as sinful, dangerous, and acceptable only within narrow confines like heterosexual marriage for procreation. This restriction doesn't just suppress our sexuality; it severs us from our own embodied wisdom.

When we're taught to view our pleasure as wrong—or worse, as something we owe to others—we lose the ability to trust ourselves. This detachment doesn't just rob us of joy; it perpetuates a culture where our bodies belong to others' expectations of what is "proper" or "holy." Reclaiming pleasure, then, is not just about sex or sensuality. It's about reclaiming ourselves—our autonomy, our desires, and the deep, intuitive wisdom our bodies hold.

Let's explore what it means to reconnect with pleasure—not as something given, withheld, or dictated by others, but as a vital part of who we are.

Pleasure: Reclaiming the Fullness of Our Senses

From an early age, women are taught that our bodies are only valuable for their capacity to bear children or satisfy a man's needs. Pleasure, especially for women, is tied to purpose: procreation, service, and duty. This narrative strips away the joy, curiosity, and expansiveness that pleasure brings to our lives.

But pleasure is not inherently sinful, nor is it something that must always look a certain way. Pleasure is essential to the human experience and is deeply tied to our sense of well-being, creativity, and spiritual growth. In this chapter, we'll explore how reclaiming pleasure in all its forms—physical, emotional, or spiritual—can help us heal from the damaging narratives of patriarchal religion and embrace a fuller, more flourishing life.

Reclaiming sexual pleasure for ourselves is not an act of selfishness—it's an act of self-love and liberation, a critical step in reconnecting with our bodies and living a life of joy and wholeness. Erotic pleasure can be a gateway to healing, satisfaction, and self-discovery. It's not simply about indulgence or physical gratification; it's about embracing the fullness of our humanity. When we experience sensuality without shame or guilt, we become more present in our skin, more connected to the world, and more deeply in tune with what brings us joy.

This reclaiming of pleasure is not a betrayal of spiritual values but a return to our inherent right to experience our bodies as our own. By exploring sensuality and erotic pleasure for our own well-being and enjoyment, we take back control from the narratives that have commodified our body's innate wisdom about what feels good and what is permissible. We settle into the natural state of our bodies, free from shame and guilt, and open ourselves to a more profound sense of satisfaction and connection with ourselves—one that transcends the limitations placed on us by exploitative patriarchal systems.

When we reclaim our right to pleasure, we reclaim our bodies, our autonomy, and our wisdom. This is not just a personal victory; it's a radical act of resistance against the systems that have sought to control us for centuries. And in doing so, we pave the way for a more liberated, joyful, and whole version of ourselves.

The Weaponization of Sex for Self-Pleasure

For centuries, patriarchal religious structures have tightly controlled pleasure, particularly non-hetero-male pleasure, framing it as dangerous, selfish, or sinful unless confined to narrow, heteronormative, cisgender marital frameworks. These teachings, rooted in patriarchal interpretations of Scripture, suggest that pleasure, especially sexual pleasure, is only valid when tied to procreation and the service of others. This belief system strips individuals—primarily women—of their right to experience pleasure for their own well-being, instead positioning their bodies as instruments of reproduction or satisfaction for others.

The concept of the "virgin" is a prime example of how women's sexuality has been distorted. Originally, the word "virgin" referred to a young, unmarried woman, with little emphasis on her sexual activity. However, over time, particularly within Christian theology, "virginity" became synonymous with sexual "purity." This shift in meaning tied a woman's worth to her sexual inexperience and weaponized her body against her autonomy. The message was clear: A woman's value diminished if she explored her sexuality or pleasure outside the confines of a heterosexual, procreative marriage.

By distorting the narrative of pleasure in this way, patriarchal systems taught women to fear their bodies and desires, pushing them to disconnect from the inherent wisdom their bodies offer. Pleasure became something that needed to be earned through submission, sacrifice, or service, while men were granted a broader range of sexual freedom. This double standard reinforced the idea that male pleasure was natural, healthy, and even celebrated, while female pleasure was suspect, sinful, and dangerous.

Self-serving pleasure, in particular, is often classified as sinful lust within Christian patriarchal culture. Anything that centers on personal joy and fulfillment rather than procreative or marital duty may be labeled as deviant or selfish. This framing shames individuals (especially women) for exploring their own desires or engaging in self-pleasure, further entrenching the control these structures seek to maintain.

The Control of Nonprocreative Pleasure and Its Consequences

These teachings extend beyond the realm of heterosexual relationships, and are often weaponized against Queer individuals and couples. Patriarchal religious systems argue that because same-sex couples cannot biologically reproduce without medical assistance, they are "unnatural." Yet this belief is not rooted in reality. Across the animal kingdom, same-sex pair-bonding and sexual behavior are widely observed in species ranging from dolphins and bonobos to birds and reptiles. These behaviors challenge the notion that procreation is the sole purpose of sexual expression, demonstrating that pleasure and connection serve broader, natural purposes.

Despite this, patriarchal systems continue to dismiss the validity of nonprocreative pleasure, whether it is same-sex relationships or self-pleasure. These frameworks attempt to control individuals by making them believe their bodies must only serve others, reinforcing the idea that autonomy and personal fulfillment are wrong or even sinful. This control, particularly over sexual and sensual pleasure, is a powerful tool for maintaining dominance over marginalized groups, keeping women and Queer individuals from living fully embodied, liberated lives.

By perpetuating guilt and shame around nonprocreative pleasure, patriarchal systems not only diminish individual autonomy but also erode the capacity for joy, self-trust, and well-being. Reclaiming sexual and self-pleasure, regardless of gender or orientation, becomes an act of defiance and liberation. It challenges the deeply ingrained structures that have sought to control bodies and desires for centuries.

Pleasure for Men versus Pleasure for Women: The Hypocrisy of Patriarchy

In modern Christian teachings, the hypocrisy surrounding pleasure is particularly glaring. Men are often permitted to experience joy and are even told that they have a stronger, more uncontrollable sexual drive, which women are expected to accommodate. Women, on the other hand, are frequently told that their bodies are dangerous, that their sensuality leads to sin, and that any pleasure they experience should be tied to serving others, particularly their husbands.

This creates a disturbing dichotomy: men are allowed to pursue pleasure, often without consequence, while women are expected to remain devoid of desire. Men's "struggles" with controlling their impulses are treated as natural and excusable. At the same time, women are warned not to "tempt" men, which leads to a denial of their own physicality, pleasure, and autonomy—reinforcing the narrative that women's bodies are the problem. This is not only harmful but profoundly unjust.

The hypocrisy here is apparent. Men's pleasure is expected, while women's pleasure is feared, a threat, and something to be controlled. This imbalance teaches women to be ashamed of their bodies, to hide their desires, and to view their sensuality as something dangerous. But true pleasure is not about serving someone else's needs. Other people may be present, but embracing pleasure is about reclaiming the joy and beauty of our own bodies and experiences.

Restoring the Expansive Definition of Pleasure

It's essential to understand that pleasure isn't confined to sexual experiences. Patriarchal systems have limited our view of pleasure, associating it primarily with sex or as something that must be "earned" through service to others. But pleasure is far more expansive. It's about tapping into the joy available to us in everyday life—the simple, sensory experiences that bring us back to ourselves.

Imagine the feeling of sinking into rest without guilt, letting your body relax without the pressure to be productive. Rest, something as basic and necessary as breathing, becomes a radical act when we reclaim it as a source of pleasure. Rest restores us, nourishes our nervous system, and brings us back to a place of balance. Yet, we are often taught to associate rest with laziness, primarily when it doesn't serve a purpose beyond recharging for more work.

Play, too, is a form of pleasure often dismissed as childish or unproductive. Play could mean dancing without care, laughing until your stomach hurts, or engaging in creative hobbies simply because they bring you joy. When was the last time you allowed yourself to play without worrying about how it might be perceived or whether it was a "good use of time"?

Food is another powerful source of pleasure that goes beyond mere sustenance. The delight of food that excites your taste buds—whether it's the sweet burst of fruit, the richness of chocolate, or the complexity of spices—can bring immense joy. Yet, in patriarchal and religious narratives, even food is viewed as something to control, as though our enjoyment of it must be restricted or tied to a strict purpose. For women, in particular, there is often shame associated with enjoying food. We are taught to deny our bodies not only nutrition but also pleasure in eating, all in the pursuit of achieving a socially acceptable physical appearance. This denial is framed as discipline, but it ultimately robs women of a fundamental source of joy and connection to our bodies.

When we expand our understanding of pleasure beyond the sexual, we allow ourselves to reconnect with our bodies and senses in ways that nourish us. These moments of joy—whether through rest, play, or food—are vital to our well-being. They ground us, offer healing, and help us reclaim the fullness of our human experience, free from shame or the need to justify our pleasure.

The Cost of Starving Ourselves of Pleasure

Humans are biologically wired to experience pleasure. It is not an indulgence but a natural and necessary part of life that supports mental, emotional, and physical well-being. Research shows that when we engage in pleasurable activities, our brain releases neurochemicals that make us feel good and play critical roles in regulating our mood, stress levels, and overall health.

For example, dopamine, often called the "feel-good" neurotransmitter, is involved in the brain's reward and pleasure systems. It's activated when we experience something enjoyable, whether that's savoring a delicious meal, playing with a pet, or laughing with a friend. Serotonin, another key neurotransmitter, helps regulate mood, sleep, and appetite and is closely linked to feelings of well-being and happiness. Endorphins, the body's natural painkillers, are released during physical activities like exercise or even laughter, reducing pain and promoting a sense of euphoria. Oxytocin, known as the "love hormone," is released through touch, social bonding, and moments of intimacy, fostering feelings of connection and trust.

However, when we deny ourselves the opportunity to experience pleasure—whether due to societal pressures, guilt, or shame—the effects can be damaging; a lack of pleasure and chronic stress can lead to various physical and emotional issues, including anxiety, depression, and weakened immune systems. In extreme cases, the absence of pleasure or positive reinforcement can lead to conditions like anhedonia, the inability to feel pleasure in activities that usually bring joy, which is a key symptom of depression.

A study conducted by neuroscientists at the University of Michigan found that animals deprived of pleasurable stimuli, such as play or social interaction, exhibited higher levels of stress hormones and showed impaired brain function over time. The same holds true for humans: When we are disconnected from pleasure, our mental, emotional, and even physical health suffers.[2]

Starving ourselves of pleasure can cause more harm than we realize. The pressure to always be productive and the guilt associated with taking time to enjoy life can lead to physical, mental, and emotional burnout. We can become stuck in patterns of self-denial, disconnected from the things that bring us joy and sustenance.

Pleasure as a State of Well-Being

At its core, pleasure is deeply intertwined with our well-being. It's not just about momentary satisfaction or physical gratification. Pleasure is about cultivating a lasting sense of connection, joy, and alignment with our true selves. When we experience pleasure—whether through creativity, stimulating conversations, or meaningful relationships—our brain releases chemicals like dopamine and endorphins that generate happiness and contentment. These neurochemical responses reduce stress, promote overall mental and emotional health, and strengthen our resilience.

Experiencing pleasure also helps our bodies by lowering cortisol levels, reducing inflammation, and improving cardiovascular health. Engaging in joyful, pleasurable activities activates the parasympathetic nervous system, allowing the body to rest, digest, and heal. This physiological response helps counterbalance the stress we face daily, grounding us in a state of well-being and relaxation.

Pleasure isn't just about fleeting moments of joy. It's about creating an ongoing sense of fulfillment, curiosity, and engagement. Activities like making art, enjoying nature, or even relishing a good meal stimulate parts of the brain associated with learning and growth, like the prefrontal cortex. These experiences increase emotional resilience and foster a deeper connection to the world around us.

When we can experience pleasure without shame or guilt, it opens the door to a profound sense of wellness and fulfillment. Many women have been conditioned to feel guilt around pleasure, particularly physical pleasure, but this shame only distances us from our bodies and our well-being. The internal conflict between desiring joy and fearing it leaves us disconnected from our senses and our full potential for happiness.

Reclaiming pleasure isn't just about enjoyment; it's about healing. It's about restoring our relationship with our bodies and recognizing that they are sacred and deserving of joy. Unabashed pleasure can heal some of the deepest wounds we carry from patriarchal conditioning, leading us to a life where well-being and fulfillment are not just possible but celebrated. By reclaiming pleasure, we take vital steps toward living a life of authenticity, joy, and wholeness.

The Revolution of Reclaiming Pleasure as Healing

Patriarchal systems, particularly within religious frameworks, have long painted women's desires and bodies as dangerous or sinful, teaching us that pleasure—especially physical pleasure—is something we must suppress, avoid, or control. This narrative goes even further, suggesting that indulging in pleasure makes us inherently flawed or somehow "against God." These harmful ideas have disconnected us from our bodies, preventing us from living fully and experiencing the joy, sensuality, and fulfillment that is our birthright.

But what if we rejected this narrative? What if we reclaimed pleasure as a fundamental human right and embraced our own wisdom and intuition as sources of power and joy? By trusting ourselves—our desires, our bodies, and our internal wisdom—we can break free from the systems that have controlled us for generations. Reclaiming pleasure is not about rejecting spirituality but about rejecting the idea that pleasure is sinful or selfish. Instead, it is a radical self-love, healing, and resistance act.

When we allow ourselves to experience pleasure—whether it's through sexual, sensual, or simple everyday joys—we reclaim autonomy over our bodies and lives. Pleasure is not just about sex. It's about engaging all of our senses, allowing ourselves to feel joy, comfort, and contentment in moments like a walk in nature, laughter with friends, or savoring a delicious meal. Pleasure can be found in the smallest details, and when we open ourselves to it, we nourish our well-being in ways that patriarchal systems have denied us.

Patriarchal religion and society have long controlled women's bodies, dictating how they should be used and experienced—primarily for the benefit of others, be it through reproduction, satisfying a partner, or caregiving. But our bodies are not vessels of duty alone. They are capable of joy, creativity, and sensuality, and reconnecting with our bodies is a powerful way to reclaim what has been taken from us. Embracing pleasure means undoing the damage caused by centuries of repression. It means seeing our bodies as sacred vessels deserving of pleasure, not objects to be controlled or shamed.

This reclamation extends beyond sexual pleasure, giving us permission to live fully and enjoy life without guilt or self-judgment. When we embrace pleasure as a basic human right, we open ourselves to the full spectrum of the human experience: physical, emotional, and spiritual. We begin to understand that our bodies are not broken or sinful but are sacred, capable of deep pleasure and joy. Rejecting the shame placed on pleasure is an essential step toward healing, helping us move out of survival mode and into a space where we can thrive.

Reclaiming pleasure is also a revolutionary act that models empowerment for future generations. It helps break the cycle of shame and repression that has been passed down through centuries of patriarchal control. By embracing pleasure in all its forms, we show our children, our communities, and ourselves that living fully—without fear or guilt—is not just possible but essential.

Finally, reclaiming pleasure is not about indulgence at the expense of others. True pleasure is about finding joy and satisfaction in ways that honor our bodies, our relationships, and the world around us. It is about living in alignment with our values and recognizing that we can embrace pleasure without harming anyone else. In doing so, we reject the systems that equate pleasure with sinfulness and reclaim our right to live fully, joyfully, and compassionately with ourselves and those we love.

By reclaiming pleasure, we reclaim our power, our bodies, and our right to live fully. This is not just an act of defiance against the systems that have oppressed us—it is an act of love. It honors the women who came before us and those who will follow in our footsteps. When we reclaim pleasure, we dismantle the narratives that taught our mothers and grandmothers to suppress their desires and endure silently. We challenge the systems that told them their worth was tied to self-denial and obedience.

In choosing to live fully and joyfully, we remember (and perhaps avenge) their struggles, affirming that the sacrifices they made were not in vain. At the same time, we set a new standard for those who come after us, showing that it is not only possible but necessary to live authentically, embrace our humanity, and celebrate life without shame. Pleasure is our birthright, and it is time we claim it as a normal, healthy aspect of a flourishing life.

Learning What's Pleasurable

Before we can ask for what we need from others—whether in intimate relationships or everyday connections—we must first learn what brings us pleasure. This is an exploration that invites curiosity, patience, and a deep willingness to discover what makes us feel alive, joyful, and fulfilled. Many women have been conditioned to prioritize the needs and desires of others over their own, leaving them disconnected from their bodies and what truly brings them joy.

To reclaim pleasure, we must start by reconnecting with ourselves. This might mean spending time alone, paying attention to the sensations and activities that bring comfort, joy, or peace. It could be as simple as noticing how much you enjoy the warmth of the sun on your skin, the pleasure of a delicious meal, or the satisfaction of engaging in a creative pursuit. Reconnecting with your body, emotions, and spirit in this way is an essential step toward understanding what truly nurtures you.

Exploring what feels good, both in the little moments and the larger experiences, allows you to cultivate a deeper connection with yourself. It's important to remember that pleasure isn't confined to one area of life—it can be physical, like enjoying a soft blanket or stretching your body; emotional, like laughing with friends; spiritual, like feeling connected to something greater than yourself; or relational, like bonding with others over shared experiences. The journey of learning what pleases you is ongoing, a practice of mindfulness and self-discovery that evolves as you do.

Asking for What You Want

Once you've taken the time to learn what brings you pleasure, the next step is learning to communicate those desires. Asking for what you want takes vulnerability and courage, especially in a world that often discourages women from voicing their needs. Sharing what makes you happy means exposing parts of yourself that may feel private or delicate, and it requires trust in those you choose to share with.

Not everyone deserves access to your innermost desires. People have to show that they are trustworthy before you open up about the things that matter most to you. It's important to recognize that there are different levels of intimacy, and some people may only be safe enough for you to share surface-level joys, like hobbies or lighthearted interests. Others may earn the trust needed for you to discuss more intimate or spiritual practices.

Setting boundaries about what you share—and with whom—is an essential part of protecting your emotional well-being. Trust is built over time, and it's okay to withhold certain aspects of yourself until you feel safe and understood. Knowing what brings you pleasure is one thing; sharing it with others who will respect and honor it is another.

When you do choose to share your needs, it can deepen your relationships. Whether it's asking for more time alone, expressing your desire for connection, or sharing a spiritual practice that fulfills you, learning to communicate your needs openly can transform how you engage with others. Relationships built on mutual respect, vulnerability, and trust allow both people to experience more joy, intimacy, and fulfillment.

Leaning In: Discovering What Feels Good

In this activity, you'll begin to reconnect with pleasure by exploring what truly brings you joy and satisfaction. The goal is to rediscover the unique ways your body, mind, and spirit experience pleasure—free from guilt, shame, or external expectations. This practice is designed to help you embrace curiosity, reconnect with your senses, and identify the simple pleasures that nourish and energize you.

Set aside 30–60 minutes when you can be uninterrupted. Choose a space that feels safe and inviting; this could be your bedroom, a cozy chair, or even outside in nature. Gather anything that makes the space feel comforting, such as a soft blanket, candles, or your favorite soothing music. Take a few deep breaths to center yourself, letting your body settle and your mind become present. Remind yourself that this time is for you, without judgment or expectation.

Start by exploring your five senses one at a time. Ask yourself:

- Touch: What textures feel comforting or luxurious to me? Try holding a soft fabric or running your fingers over something textured, like a smooth stone.
- Sight: What colors, images, or sights make me feel calm or joyful? Look at a piece of art, a natural view, or even a candle's flickering flame.
- Sound: What sounds bring me peace or energize me? Listen to a favorite song, the sound of water, or complete silence.
- Taste: What flavors bring me joy? Savor something simple yet delightful, like a piece of fruit, chocolate, or tea.
- Smell: What scents evoke happiness or comfort? Inhale an essential oil, the scent of a flower, or something familiar like fresh coffee or a favorite lotion.

Notice how each sense responds. Write down any observations about what feels good, what excites you, or what soothes you.

Reflect on activities, memories, or moments that have brought you pleasure in the past. Ask yourself:

- When was the last time I felt truly joyful or satisfied?
- What hobbies or activities make me lose track of time?
- What small daily moments feel comforting or fulfilling?

Jot down a few ideas, no matter how simple or indulgent they seem. For example, it could be dancing in your living room, reading a book, soaking in a bath, or enjoying a spontaneous conversation with a friend.

From your reflections, pick one source of pleasure to intentionally focus on for the next few days. It could be something new or a familiar joy you've neglected. Commit to engaging with it daily, even in small ways. For example:

- If you enjoy music, take a few minutes each day to dance, sing, or listen deeply.
- If you love nature, schedule a short walk or spend time observing the sky, trees, or flowers.
- If food is a source of pleasure, try cooking or savoring a favorite meal without distractions.

After you spend time doing something that brings you joy, take a few moments to reflect in your journal:

- How did it feel to reconnect with pleasure?
- Did any feelings of guilt, shame, or resistance come up?
- How did this practice impact your mood, energy, or sense of well-being?

Celebrate the steps you've taken, no matter how small you may think they are. Recognize that reclaiming pleasure is a process, and each moment of joy is a radical act of self-love. If you didn't like something, you can get curious about why it didn't land and then decide if you want to push past the resistance or if it's a hard stop.

Consider adding more activities to your "pleasure menu" over time. Allow your curiosity to guide you in discovering new ways to nurture your body, mind, and spirit. The more you reconnect with your senses and desires, the more deeply you'll reclaim your capacity for joy, fulfillment, and wholeness. This activity is about giving yourself permission to embrace pleasure without justification. Remember, pleasure isn't selfish—it's essential to your well-being. Reclaiming it is an act of liberation and self-love.

Chapter 6

Feeling Things

Maybe it started when you were five, and you cried because your favorite toy broke. Instead of comfort, you heard, "Stop being dramatic." Or maybe you were ten, furious about a friend who betrayed you, and someone told you, "Good girls don't get angry." By the time you were a teenager, you might have learned to smile through disappointment, to hide your frustration, and to cry quietly where no one could see. You learned that some emotions—like patience or kindness—were acceptable, but others, like anger, ambition, or even deep grief, were better left unspoken.

If this sounds familiar, it's because many of us have been taught to shrink our emotional selves into a tidy, manageable package. In patriarchal Christian contexts, women are often given permission to feel, but only within limits. Compassion, nurturance, and softness are welcomed, even celebrated, because they align with a role of service. But other emotions—ones that might disrupt that role, like desire, anger, envy, or fear—are labeled as sinful, selfish, or dangerous.

The cost of this emotional suppression runs deep. It disconnects us from ourselves, creating a divide between what we truly feel and what we allow ourselves to express. It undermines our ability to trust our own experiences, making us second-guess whether what we're feeling is valid or "allowed." Worse, it keeps us small, holding back the emotions that could drive us toward change, healing, and wholeness.

Imagine what it would be like to feel everything freely—to reclaim the parts of your emotional landscape that you've been told are too much or too messy. Together, let's explore how patriarchal systems have used emotional suppression as a tool of control and begin to chart a path toward emotional wholeness. Because your emotions—every single one of them—are not flaws to fix. They're powerful messengers, vital guides to a life that feels fully your own.

No, You're Not Being Dramatic

In patriarchal Christian contexts, women might be given a little more leeway to express emotions than men, but only within narrow confines. The emotions women are encouraged to show—like patience, nurturance, and compassion—are those that conveniently reinforce a role of quiet service to others. But as soon as we show emotions that disrupt this image—like ambition, desire, or especially anger—the labels start piling up: manipulative, rebellious, even mentally ill. Other emotions like grief, shame, fear, disappointment, and envy are also pushed into the shadows, creating a deep disconnection from perfectly normal emotions.

You're not imagining the issue. Research shows when women express "female-typed emotions, they are judged as overly emotional and lacking emotional control, all of which were used to undermine professional legitimacy."[1] These labels don't come out of nowhere; they're meant to make us feel small, meant to make us shrink back into the box that patriarchy's prepared for us, holding back any emotion that could challenge its grip on our minds, our spirits, and our bodies.

This chapter is here to help you reclaim every part of your emotional landscape—to explore what it feels like when you're free to feel *every* emotion, even the ones you've been told are wrong or dangerous. We'll look at the actual costs of emotional suppression—not just for ourselves but for our communities and the generations that come after us. Together, we'll go deep into the steps toward reclaiming emotional wholeness, a path to freedom essential for taking back our autonomy in all areas of life.

Emotions, Hysteria, and Bad Science

The fear of women's emotions runs deep in history. Women's emotional expressions have long been used as evidence of "hysteria" or mental weakness. The term "hysteria," rooted in the Greek word *hystera* (meaning "uterus"), was based on the belief that a woman's emotions were caused by a wandering womb, making them inherently unstable and irrational. This pseudoscientific idea persisted for centuries, often serving as justification for controlling women. During the Victorian era, women expressing too much passion, ambition, or anger were frequently labeled as "hysterical" and subjected to oppressive treatments, ranging from forced rest cures to institutionalization.[2]

One notable example is the case of Charlotte Perkins Gilman, whose semi-autobiographical short story *The Yellow Wallpaper* (1892) illustrates the devastating impact of Victorian Dr. S. Weir Mitchell's "rest cure," a common treatment for hysteria. Gilman's protagonist is confined to a room and forbidden from engaging in intellectual or creative pursuits, reflecting how patriarchal medical providers dismissed women's emotional expressions as illnesses to be "fixed" rather than acknowledged or understood. Gilman later explained that this treatment method nearly drove her to madness during her own season of postpartum depression. The story shares the thoughts of a woman forced to "rest" while her symptoms are downplayed and she is denied help. The tremendous harm caused by the pathologization of women's emotions and a male-driven medical system are apparent in Gilman's personal experience and the tragic decline of her story's main character.[3]

This harmful framing of women's emotionality extended far beyond Victorian medicine. For centuries, any display of "excessive" emotion—whether anger, grief, or ambition—was used as evidence to silence or control women. In the late nineteenth century, Sigmund Freud's early theories further perpetuated these ideas by tying hysteria to suppressed sexuality, framing women's emotional expression as inherently pathological and reinforcing societal narratives that devalued their experiences.

Today, we still live with the echoes of this harmful history. How often are women's emotions dismissed as "hormonal" or "irrational"? How many times have you been told to "calm down" or "not be so emotional"? This legacy of dismissal still influences how we view ourselves. When we internalize the message that our emotions are "too much," it weakens our ability to trust our feelings.

Imagine what would happen if we completely discarded the idea of "too muchness"—if we started to see our emotions as wisdom instead of weakness. This shift could change not only how we see ourselves but also how we interact with the world around us. Reconnecting to our emotions is reconnecting with who we were always created to be.

Suppression of women's emotions is also about keeping us from our inner wisdom. For centuries, any woman who showed too much wisdom, independence, or intuition was labeled "witch," "mad," or "untrustworthy." From the witch hunts of history to politics today, women who express beyond a narrow range of emotions are seen as dangerous.

This isn't a coincidence. Emotions like anger, desire, and ambition are deeply connected to our power and our inner knowing. When we're encouraged to hold them back, we become dependent on external validation for our decision-making.

Patriarchal systems rely on us questioning ourselves and seeing our emotions as unreliable or untrustworthy. By keeping us disconnected from our emotions, these systems ensure we remain disconnected from our inner wisdom. Connection to our emotional selves gives us back our authority, and that's what patriarchal systems fear most.

But what would happen if we reclaimed this wisdom? By fully feeling everything we feel, we open the door to deeper intuition, stronger boundaries, and a kind of self-knowledge that patriarchy cannot control. We begin to see that our emotions are not only valid—they're essential.

When we dare to let ourselves feel everything, we align with the countercultural women labeled witchy or dangerous. We're saying, "I refuse to shrink myself to fit your expectations." It's a radical act, a stand for our wholeness and autonomy. It's not about seeking confrontation just to pick a fight but about reconnecting to a power that's always been ours—the power to feel, to know, and to trust ourselves.

Why Are Some Emotions Off-Limits?

Have you ever noticed how some emotions feel off-limits, like they belong to a "don't go there" category? Most of us have felt that nudge, whether spoken or silent, to "tone it down," "stay pleasant," or "not make a fuss." It's not just about being polite. There's something much bigger at play. When we're encouraged only to feel certain emotions and avoid others, it's easier for those around us to manage us. This suppression is no accident; Christian patriarchy constrains emotion as a control mechanism, telling us which emotions are acceptable and which are sinful or will "make trouble." It's like they're creating a script we're supposed to follow that keeps us disconnected from ourselves and each other.

Christian teachings that prioritize submission and gentleness above all else leave women feeling unworthy or spiritually inadequate when they experience emotions outside of these approved expressions. This creates a spiritual alienation that disconnects women from their own inner wisdom, intuition, and direct experience of the Divine. When emotions are viewed as unholy or dangerous, women are left questioning our spiritual value and purpose, further entrenching cycles of guilt and shame.

Here are a few ways women's emotional expression is judged by patriarchal society:

- Anger: Seen as "hysterical" or "irrational," anger in women challenges expectations of gentleness.
- Ambition: Women are shamed for ambition, often labeled "selfish" or "bossy."
- Desire: Expressing personal or sexual desire invites judgment as "promiscuous" or "unfeminine."
- Assertiveness: Assertive women are seen as "demanding" or "domineering."
- Grief: Prolonged grief is dismissed as dramatic or attention-seeking.
- Sadness: Excessive sadness leads to labels like "weak" or "overly sensitive."
- Frustration: Frustration is reframed as "nagging" or being "difficult."
- Confidence: Confident women are accused of being "arrogant" or "vain."
- Rage: Rage is labeled as "dangerous" or "out of control" when expressed by women.
- Envy: Envy is seen as "petty" or "jealous" rather than human.
- Disappointment: Disappointment is dismissed as "overly critical" or "too sensitive."
- Pride: Pride is seen as "conceited" or "vain" in women.
- Independence: Emotional independence is labeled as "cold" or "aloof."

Patriarchal systems, especially those rooted in religious authority, rely on us playing the roles they assign us. When we're told to stick to "positive" emotions like joy, patience, and gentleness, it's not because these are the only emotions normal humans should feel. It's because they make us more predictable and controllable. Patriarchy feels safe when we're compliant, but it starts to feel a little shaky when we step outside our comfort zone. Expressing anger or frustration disrupts these systems, reminding everyone, including ourselves, that our feelings have power.

The Cost of Emotional Suppression

So what happens when certain feelings are considered off-limits? Emotional suppression has a way of impacting us deeply, touching every part of our lives, from our health to our relationships and even our spiritual lives. It creates a constant need to "be strong," which often translates into walking on eggshells around our own emotions, stuffing them down, and pretending they don't matter.

For example, in Christian patriarchal households, women are often expected to remain the "emotional caretakers," soothing others' feelings while hiding our own anger or discontent. The result is a relationship where only one person's emotional needs are met—typically the man's, while the woman's emotional landscape is ignored or minimized. Even emotions like tiredness or stress are dismissed because women are expected to "keep it together." Over time, this dynamic creates deep emotional dissatisfaction, leaving women feeling disconnected from other partners, their friends, and even themselves.

When emotions like anger or assertiveness are off-limits, we often find ourselves in relationships where we are unable to assert boundaries or demand respect. Without the full spectrum of emotions at our disposal, women's relationships remain limited, often shallow, and unfulfilling. We are forced to suppress our true feelings while performing emotional labor that leaves us depleted and feeling disconnected.

The truth is, emotional suppression doesn't make us stronger—it keeps us disconnected, making us more vulnerable to stress and further isolating us from our bodies, our resilience, and each other.

- *Relational impact*: When we suppress emotions, especially ones like anger or frustration, it affects our relationships. Instead of speaking up, we hold back, and resentment builds quietly. Imagine being in a relationship where you can't ever express dissatisfaction or boundaries without feeling guilty. Over time, this leads to distance. When one person's emotions are hidden or minimized, there's a limit on how deep that relationship can go. How many times have you felt the need to "keep the peace" by swallowing your emotions?
- *Physical impact*: Emotional suppression doesn't just stay in our minds. It also lives in our bodies. When we don't express emotions, we often carry them as physical tension and, over time, this can lead to headaches, digestive issues, fatigue, and even more serious health problems. Think about it—how often do you feel stress in your shoulders, your stomach, or your chest? That's your body holding onto emotions that need to be felt, expressed, and let go. By staying connected to our feelings, we can stay connected to our bodies, honoring what they need to feel, process, and heal.
- *Spiritual impact*: Patriarchy loves to tell us which emotions are "holy" and which are "sinful." Emotions like anger, desire, or ambition are often painted as

dangerous or sinful. We're encouraged to filter these feelings through male leaders or, worse, to ignore them entirely. This disconnects us from our inner wisdom. When we're told our emotions are unworthy of divine acknowledgment, it leaves us questioning our spiritual value. Imagine what it would be like to fully trust that all your feelings are valid and sacred, that they're part of your connection to the Divine.

Gatekeeping Emotions Deflects Accountability

Another reason patriarchal culture suppresses emotions is that it's easier to dismiss someone's emotional experience than to take responsibility for the harm or discomfort that caused it. When women express emotions like anger or disappointment, especially in response to being wronged, those responsible are forced to confront their actions.

Taking accountability for causing pain or discomfort requires an ego hit that many are unwilling to endure. Dismissing these emotions as irrational or exaggerated is far simpler than addressing the underlying issues. By pushing women to disconnect from these emotions, society allows those in power to evade responsibility, perpetuating the cycle of harm without consequence. In this way, emotional suppression controls the individual and protects the egos of those responsible for causing harm.

Women are pressured to dissociate from the full spectrum of their emotions because their emotional freedom disrupts control systems, challenges the vulnerability of those in power, and forces accountability for the harm caused. This pressure to dissociate is a deliberate mechanism to uphold oppressive structures, ensuring that those in power remain protected from the emotional consequences of their actions. When reclaiming the full range of emotions, women challenge these systems and begin to dismantle the barriers that keep them oppressed.

The Gift of Emotional Availability

So, what happens when we make room for our full emotional range? Reclaiming emotional wholeness isn't just about rejecting old beliefs. It's about healing, about stepping back into our full, vibrant, emotional selves. When we honor our emotions, we start healing our connection to our bodies, minds, and spirits. This connection increases resilience, grounding us so that we're able to weather the storms that come our way. Emotional availability is transformative, touching every part of our lives—from how we relate to ourselves to how deeply we connect with others and even how we experience our spirituality.

When we welcome our emotions, instead of shutting them down, we step into a state of openness and authenticity that's healing, grounding, and empowering. Emotional availability isn't a vulnerability to be hidden—it's a powerful form of resilience that roots us deeply in our bodies, strengthens our connections, and enriches our spiritual lives.

- *Personal impact*: When we allow ourselves to be fully available to our emotions, we begin to see and accept ourselves more completely. This doesn't mean living at the whim of every feeling that comes up; it's about having a strong, healthy connection to what we truly feel. Think about it—How much energy do we spend pushing feelings down or convincing ourselves that our needs don't matter? Emotional availability helps us tune in to what's really going on, leading to a stronger sense of self and clearer boundaries. This honest connection builds resilience, empowering us to face life's challenges with clarity and strength rather than the stress of holding things in. Imagine being able to acknowledge every emotion without fear or judgment, knowing that each one has value and a role in guiding you.

- *Relational impact*: When we're emotionally available to ourselves, we open doors to deeper, more meaningful relationships. When we're open about our feelings, we invite empathy, trust, and genuine intimacy, creating an environment where everyone feels safe to show up as their authentic selves. Have you noticed the tension that rises up when you want to speak up, share your truth, or set a boundary but feel the need to "keep things light"? Emotional availability lets us communicate honestly, stand steady during conflicts, and show up fully in our relationships, making space for both the joys and the challenges. Imagine how freeing it would be to connect with others who value all of you, even when they disagree or don't understand.
- *Spiritual impact*: Embracing emotional availability also deepens our spiritual lives. We're more open to experiencing the sacred in each moment when we welcome our emotions rather than dismissing them. Patriarchy often tells us which emotions are "holy" and which are "sinful," pushing us to limit what we allow ourselves to feel in spiritual spaces. But emotional availability opens us to a fuller experience of the Divine—letting us bring our whole selves to our spiritual journey, not just the "approved" parts. Imagine feeling a deep connection to your spirituality where every emotion is acknowledged as valid, each one part of your path to understanding, connection, growth, and spiritual flourishing. When we honor our emotions, we also honor our sacred connection to the universe, to others, and to ourselves.

Embracing our emotions gives us access to strength we might not have realized we had. When we stop suppressing emotions, we start living in a way that honors our boundaries, our desires, and our voice. We realize that real strength isn't about stuffing down what we feel; it's about fully engaging with it and building resilience by staying deeply connected to our inner experience.

Imagine a world where you could fully embrace every part of your emotional life. Where no emotion was off-limits, and every feeling had a place at the table. Reclaiming emotional wholeness doesn't just change us; it changes everything around us. We become connected in ways we never imagined—to ourselves, to each other, to something beyond us. If we, as women, allow ourselves to step into the fullness of our emotional truth, we not only reclaim our power, we create communities that honor and celebrate every part of who we are.

Creating Supportive Environments for Emotional Growth

To fully embrace emotional wholeness, it's essential to cultivate internal and external environments that support your emotional growth. Shifting the way you interact with yourself and others, as well as how you engage with your emotions, can create space for healing and help you move away from the shame or misogyny that has often surrounded "certain feelings." By fostering environments where you feel safe to explore your full emotional range, you create the foundation for emotional well-being and the trust necessary to reconnect with your inner knowing.

One of the most important shifts you can make is allowing yourself the time and space to gradually reclaim suppressed or discouraged emotions. This isn't about forcing yourself to express emotions you're not ready for but about creating a gentle process of reintroduction. By starting small, you build confidence in your emotional expression, making it easier to integrate suppressed feelings over time.

For example, if anger is off-limits for you, find low-stakes situations where you can practice assertiveness. This might mean setting a boundary in a casual interaction or expressing frustration in a way that feels manageable. The key is to acknowledge that these emotions are valid and allow yourself the opportunity to express them in small ways.

By starting small, you create space for emotional balance to grow gradually. This approach fosters self-compassion as you reconnect with emotions that have been pushed away, allowing them to surface without overwhelming you.

The idea that women are too emotional (rather than "logical"), or too connected to our bodies (instead of dependent on external validation for our decisions) has served as justification for blocking us from positions of power, both in spiritual and secular settings. Women's emotions have been painted as a liability rather than a source of wisdom, reinforcing the notion that male authority is needed to keep society stable.

By reclaiming these suppressed emotions, women create space for emotional, relational, and spiritual healing. When women allow themselves to experience emotions like rage, ambition, or desire, we are no longer constrained by patriarchal teachings that label these emotions as dangerous. Instead, we recognize these emotions as essential aspects of our humanity and divine wisdom.

Reclaiming emotional wholeness leads to a more integrated and holistic sense of self. It allows women to reconnect with our bodies, which often hold onto suppressed emotions, and release the physical tension that comes from emotional repression. It also opens the door to deeper spiritual connections, as women are no longer bound by the belief that only certain emotions are worthy of divine acknowledgment.

Creating Space for Feelings

Making a conscious effort to express a range of emotions regularly is critical to emotional growth. Many of us have been conditioned to suppress certain emotions or only express "socially acceptable" ones like happiness or gratitude. However, to develop emotional wholeness, it's important to give yourself permission to express all of your emotions, including sadness, anger, frustration, or even ambition.

Creating space for emotional expression might mean scheduling time to check in with yourself each day. Ask, "What am I feeling right now?" and "What emotion am I resisting?" If tears come up, let yourself cry without judgment. If you feel a surge of ambition or excitement about a new goal, allow yourself to celebrate that feeling, even if you've been taught it's "selfish" or "unladylike."

Regular emotional expression normalizes emotions that were once off-limits, builds emotional fluency, and helps you integrate them as a natural part of your life.

Emotional awareness is the foundation of emotional growth. Many of us move through life disconnected from our feelings simply because we've been taught not to pay attention to them. Developing awareness means checking in with yourself and recognizing your emotions as they arise.

One way to cultivate emotional awareness is through journaling. Take time each day to write down how you're feeling—whether it's an emotion that's easy for you to express or one that feels more difficult. Use the feeling wheel at the end of this chapter to explore new names for feelings that were off-limits earlier in life. This practice can reveal patterns and help you see where certain emotions have been suppressed or ignored. Ask yourself questions like, "What emotion am I feeling right now?" and "How is this emotion showing up in my body?"

By regularly checking in with yourself, you develop a clearer understanding of your emotional landscape. This self-awareness creates the foundation for deeper emotional balance as you become more attuned to how your feelings impact your body and mind.

Cultivating Supportive Relationships: Surrounding Yourself with Emotional Safety

The people you surround yourself with majorly affect your emotional growth. If you've spent time in environments where emotions were suppressed or judged, seeking out new relationships where your full emotional range is welcomed and respected is essential.

Cultivating supportive relationships starts with being open about your own emotions. Share your feelings with trusted friends, family members, or partners who encourage emotional openness. This creates an atmosphere where vulnerability is not only allowed but celebrated. When you're in spaces that encourage emotional honesty, you'll find it easier to explore and express a broader range of emotions without fear of judgment or dismissal.

Look for people who celebrate your joy but also hold space for your anger, sadness, or frustration. Building these supportive environments allows you to grow emotionally and heal from past suppression.

Engaging in Physical Practices: Connecting Body and Emotion

Emotions don't live just in the mind—we're deeply connected to the body. Often, emotions that we've suppressed for years manifest as physical tension, pain, or illness. That's why engaging in physical practices that allow emotional release is a powerful way to support emotional growth.

Yoga, dance, breathwork, self-pleasure, and other movement-based practices can help you reconnect with your emotions on a physical level. Set aside time each day to move intuitively—whether it's a short walk, stretching, or dancing to your favorite music. As you move, notice where emotions show up in your body and allow yourself to release any tension that's tied to them.

By engaging in regular physical practices, you'll develop a deeper connection to your body's emotional wisdom. This allows emotions to flow through you naturally instead of getting stuck or suppressed, leading to greater emotional balance. Remember, you can always go back to the activity you learned at the end of chapter 1 when you need help reconnecting with your body.

Rewriting Your Emotional Story: Letting Go of Shame

Many of us carry stories about emotions that have been passed down through patriarchal and cultural systems. We've been taught that certain emotions are "bad" or "selfish" or that expressing ourselves makes us unworthy. Rewriting your emotional story means letting go of these narratives and embracing the full spectrum of your emotional life without shame.

Start by identifying the stories you've been told about emotions like anger, desire, or sadness. Who told you these stories? Why were these emotions labeled as unacceptable or dangerous? Once you've identified the roots of these stories, begin letting go.

One way to rewrite your emotional story is through self-compassion. When you feel an emotion rising that you've been taught to suppress, remind yourself that this feeling is valid. Practice affirmations like, "I have the right to feel anger," or "My desires are sacred." Over time, this practice will help you shed the shame that's been attached to certain feelings, allowing you to embrace emotional wholeness.

By creating supportive environments that nurture your emotional growth, you'll strengthen your connection to your inner knowing and begin to trust your emotions rather than suppressing them. Emotional wholeness doesn't happen overnight, but with time, patience, and intention you'll unlock the full range of your emotional life and step into your power as a whole, authentic being.

Embodying Emotional Wholeness

Reclaiming emotional wholeness is a journey of liberation. When we honor the full range of our feelings, we're stepping into a world where we're free to be whole. We're not seeking permission but reclaiming what's always been ours.

This journey is about more than just personal healing. It's about building communities that value each person's emotional truth. When we reclaim our emotional wholeness, we're laying the groundwork for a world where everyone's emotions are honored, and our feelings lead us toward freedom and connection.

Imagine stepping into your life fully alive, fully embodied, and fully feeling. That's the power of emotional wholeness—it's yours to claim, and it's here, waiting for you.

Leaning In: Unlocking Your Emotions

This activity invites you to explore the full range of emotions you experience (or don't) using a printable feelings wheel as a guide. It's designed to help you reflect on the emotions you were encouraged to feel growing up and the ones that were suppressed or discouraged. By examining these patterns, you can identify where emotional gaps exist in your life and begin the process of reclaiming your emotional wholeness.

Step 1: Print the Feelings Wheel and Gather Your Supplies

First, download and print a feelings wheel—a circular chart that displays a broad range of emotions, often organized by core feelings like joy, anger, fear, and sadness, with more nuanced emotions radiating outward.[4] Once you have it in front of you, grab two colored highlighters or markers.

Step 2: Reflect on Your Childhood Emotional Environment

Before diving into the activity, take a few moments to reflect on the emotional environment you grew up in. What emotions were praised, celebrated, or encouraged? What feelings were tolerated but perhaps not fully welcomed? Were there emotions that were simply off-limits or even drew punishment? This reflection will help prepare you for the next steps.

Step 3: Highlight the Emotions That Were Actively Encouraged

Take one of your highlighters and begin to mark the emotions on the feelings wheel that were actively encouraged during your upbringing. These could be emotions like joy, gratitude, or calmness—feelings that were celebrated or rewarded. Think of situations where you were praised for being "happy," "grateful," or "good-natured," even though that was not what you felt on the inside. Highlight these emotions in the first color.

As you go through this, notice if certain patterns emerge. Are the encouraged emotions primarily positive or "easy" emotions? Were difficult or messy emotions like anger or fear discouraged? Were you perhaps encouraged to be compliant, pleasant, or polite at all times?

Step 4: Highlight the Emotions That Were Tolerated

Now, take the second highlighter and mark the emotions that were tolerated in your upbringing but not necessarily welcomed with open arms. These might be emotions like sadness, mild frustration, or fear—feelings that were acknowledged but perhaps minimized or brushed aside. They were acceptable to express in small doses but not something you could dwell on for long periods.

As you highlight these tolerated emotions, think back to specific memories. Were there times you were allowed to feel sad or disappointed, but only if you didn't "make a fuss" or stayed quiet? Were you given space to express frustration, but only if it wasn't too loud or disruptive?

Step 5: Reflect on the Unmarked Emotions—Those That Were Suppressed

Now, look at the emotions on the wheel that remain uncolored. These are the emotions that were largely off-limits for you growing up. These might include anger, rage, desire, ambition, or even sackcloth-and-ashes-level grief. These emotions represent areas of your emotional life that were suppressed or never given room to breathe.

Sit with these unmarked emotions for a few moments. Why were they discouraged or suppressed? What messages did you receive about these emotions? Were you taught that expressing anger made you "unladylike" or that ambition made you "selfish"? Did you believe that feeling desire or longing was inappropriate? This is a crucial part of the process because your emotional growth can begin in these uncolored spaces.

Step 6: Journal or Meditate on the Suppressed Emotions

Grab your journal or find a quiet place to meditate to deepen your reflection. Reflect on these uncolored, suppressed emotions. What would it look like to welcome these into your life now? How might embracing them change your relationships, your sense of self, or your spiritual journey?

Journaling prompts might include:

- What would it feel like to express anger or frustration without guilt or shame?
- How can I begin to honor emotions like ambition, desire, or rage more freely?

- What might I need to let go of (beliefs, fears, judgments) to fully embrace these off-limits emotions?

This reflection can be emotional and sometimes uncomfortable, but it's an important step in reclaiming parts of yourself that have been hidden or silenced for too long.

Chapter 7

Governing Self

Throughout this journey, we've explored the deep-rooted ways Christian patriarchy has shaped the roles, rights, and spiritual experiences of women. Nowhere is this more apparent than in the issue of self-governance. Christian patriarchal teachings often promote the idea that men are divinely ordained to have authority over women, framing this as necessary for women's protection. Yet, this concept is at odds with Jesus's message of liberation for all.

Autonomy is not simply the ability to make decisions—it is the gateway to feminine wisdom, enabling women to trust their intuition, draw on their creativity, and lead with empathy in ways that reflect their full, authentic selves. In this chapter, we explore why Christian patriarchy opposes female autonomy, how its control impacts women, and how reclaiming self-governance is a vital step toward liberating ourselves.

Why Christian Patriarchy Opposes Female Autonomy

We've already spent significant time discussing the historical context of male authority in Christianity. The Genesis narrative, particularly Eve's role in the fall of humanity, has long been weaponized to suggest that women's pursuit of wisdom is dangerous and disruptive. Eve's choice to eat from the Tree of Knowledge has been portrayed as the reason for humanity's downfall, painting women as temptresses in need of control. This association between female wisdom and danger set the stage for centuries of teachings that degrade women's ability to govern their own lives.

The suppression of women's autonomy is ultimately a suppression of feminine wisdom—intuition, empathy, and relational insight—that has long been dismissed as a threat to hierarchical control. Paul's letters, particularly passages like Ephesians 5:22–24 and 1 Timothy 2:12–14, have reinforced this idea, insisting that women must submit to male authority in religious and domestic life. Early Christian theologians like Augustine and Tertullian argued that women's wisdom was inherently inferior. This mindset created a culture that actively discourages women from trusting their own bodies, intellect, and spiritual instincts.

The heart of Christian patriarchy's opposition to female autonomy lies in its fear of disruption. Women who govern themselves—who trust their own wisdom and assert their authority—threaten the very fabric of a male-dominated society. Autonomy disrupts the control patriarchal systems have maintained for centuries, particularly over women's bodies and spirituality. Women's reproductive autonomy, for example, undermines the patriarchy's power over women's roles within the family and society.

Women who know and confidently express what they want are seen as particularly dangerous. The self-governed woman symbolizes a broader reclaiming of women's wisdom and power. If women are trusted to lean into their own wisdom, trust what they know to be true, and govern every aspect of their lives, patriarchal religious teachings lose their control. This is why Christian patriarchy works so hard to suppress female autonomy—because it knows that once women embrace their own power, the systems that have long controlled them will begin to crumble.

The Impact of Patriarchal Control of Women's Autonomy

Christian patriarchy's control over women's autonomy has a deep, lasting impact on our self-esteem, confidence, and sense of self-trust. By constantly reinforcing the message that women's wisdom and decision-making abilities are inherently inferior to men's, these systems plant the seeds of self-doubt and breed insecurity. We grow up internalizing the belief that we cannot trust ourselves, that our perspectives are unreliable, and that we need external (often male) validation to navigate life's decisions.

Patriarchal systems sever women from their inner wisdom, leaving them disconnected from the intuitive knowing that often guides their relationships, decisions, and spiritual practices. Reclaiming autonomy is an act of restoring trust in that wisdom, allowing women to navigate life with clarity and confidence.

Constant undermining of a woman's ability to self-govern leads to widespread feelings of self-doubt and diminished confidence. Many of us come to believe that our instincts and choices are flawed, pushing us to second-guess ourselves in every sphere—whether it's making decisions about our careers, personal lives, or spiritual practices. This erosion of self-confidence keeps women trapped in cycles of hesitation and overreliance on male authority figures like fathers, husbands, or pastors. Instead of trusting our inner voice, we are conditioned to defer to others, further diminishing our sense of agency.

Limiting beliefs around autonomy and self-trust take root early. These beliefs manifest as thoughts like "I can't make this decision without someone else's input," or "I'm not capable of handling this on my own." Over time, this conditioning results in a persistent fear of failure and a reluctance to take risks or embrace new opportunities. Many women in Christian patriarchal settings are taught to see themselves as spiritually immature, in need of male guidance to navigate their faith, their emotions, and even their everyday lives. This strategy of disconnection from our inner knowing severs women from themselves, ensuring that we remain isolated, cautious of our inner voices, and wary of forming bonds that might disrupt the patriarchal structure.

Studies have shown that these harmful messages—wrapped in the guise of benevolent sexism, which suggests that male authority is there to protect women—actually undermine women's self-esteem and foster a damaging dependency on male approval.[1] This emotional and psychological harm runs deep, eroding women's ability to make decisions confidently, trust their wisdom, or act in alignment with their true desires.

In relationships, patriarchal teachings foster power imbalances, leading to emotional and relational dissatisfaction. Christian marriage counseling that insists on male leadership often overlooks women's physical, emotional, and spiritual needs. These partnerships are not based on mutual respect or shared decision-making but on the assumption that women must always defer to husbands, fathers, or adult male children. As a result, many women in such relationships feel disconnected, dissatisfied, and unheard.

Disconnected Souls

Perhaps the most damaging consequence of patriarchal control is spiritual alienation. Many women today report feeling spiritually drained and disconnected, particularly in evangelical and fundamentalist contexts. Traditional religious settings often require women to filter their faith through male leaders, leaving little room for personal spiritual exploration or leadership. This model fosters dependency on male authority and limits direct experiences of the Divine, perpetuating the cycles of control that patriarchal systems rely upon.

This sense of alienation is not an isolated issue; it reflects a broader trend. Recent studies reveal that nearly 40 percent of Generation Z women now identify as religiously unaffiliated, a sharp increase compared to previous generations.[2] Historically, women have been more likely than men to remain active in religious communities, contributing significantly to their growth and vitality. However, the growing disaffiliation among women suggests deep dissatisfaction with patriarchal structures, limited leadership opportunities, and the inability to reconcile faith with contemporary social values.[3]

In stark contrast, female-led spiritual movements, often marginalized or labeled heretical, have historically provided women with spaces of profound connection, empowerment, and renewal. These movements bypass male gatekeepers and allow women to experience the sacred directly, unfiltered by institutional hierarchies. For example, the Beguines of medieval Europe formed lay spiritual communities outside the male-dominated church. These women rejected traditional roles by living independently and engaging in theological writing, charity, and direct mystical experiences of God. Although often accused of heresy, their movement provided a powerful model of female-led spirituality and autonomy, disrupting patriarchal religious norms.[4]

Similarly, Indigenous North American traditions have long honored the spiritual leadership of women such as the Iroquois Clan Mothers, who hold political and spiritual authority within their communities. Clan Mothers are responsible for upholding spiritual practices, resolving disputes, and maintaining harmony, demonstrating the integration of spiritual wisdom and leadership in societies where women's voices are central.[5]

In nineteenth-century West Africa, Kimpa Vita, a Kongolese prophetess, founded the Antonian movement, blending Christian and traditional Kongolese beliefs. Kimpa Vita preached that women had direct access to the Divine and could lead spiritual renewal within their communities. Her teachings challenged colonial and patriarchal interpretations of Christianity, providing a vision of spirituality that remains influential in decolonial discourse today.[6]

The contrast between these empowering movements and the current spiritual disconnection reported by many women highlights the need for spaces that allow women to lead, connect, and experience the Divine on their own terms. When women are denied the opportunity to explore their own spiritual paths, they are cut off from a vital source of connection, autonomy, and renewal. By reclaiming the examples set by these movements, women today can challenge the structures that alienate them and create spiritual communities rooted in empowerment, wholeness, and direct communion with the sacred.

Patriarchal structures within evangelical churches often promote a narrow vision of what is considered "good" and "godly" for women, leading to widespread spiritual disconnection. Women's ministries in these settings typically emphasize traditional roles centered on submission, service, and domestic responsibilities. While these teachings may offer some a sense of community, for many women, they leave little room for personal spiritual growth, leadership, or autonomy.

The messaging within many women's ministries reinforces this disconnection. By framing women's primary spiritual roles as caretakers, helpers, or submissive wives, these spaces teach that a woman's value lies in serving others rather than fostering a direct relationship with the Divine. For women who do not fit these roles—whether single, childless, Queer, or professionally ambitious—this limited vision often leads to feelings of guilt, shame, and spiritual inadequacy. Over time, these women may feel alienated not only from their religious communities but also from their own sense of spirituality.

Additionally, these ministries often discourage women from expressing emotions like anger, ambition, or frustration—feelings that might challenge the status quo. Instead, they are encouraged to display patience, gentleness, and self-sacrifice, which are framed as "godly feminine" virtues. This suppression of natural emotional expression can lead to a profound sense of disconnect from one's inner self and intuition.

A recent report highlights how young women, in particular, are struggling to reconcile these teachings with their personal values. Only one third of Gen Z women, for example, agree with the statement: "most churches and religious congregations treat men and women equally."[7] As more young women push back against restrictive gender roles, traditional evangelical teachings increasingly feel outdated and unrelatable.

When churches fail to adapt or offer alternative models of spirituality, they inadvertently push women away. The absence of robust leadership opportunities or space for theological exploration compounds this disconnection, leaving many women spiritually drained. Research suggests that this growing trend of disaffiliation is directly tied to the lack of meaningful engagement and representation for women within church structures.[8]

By continuing to teach a limited vision of spirituality for women, many evangelical churches perpetuate cycles of disconnection and alienation. Breaking this cycle requires a radical reimagining of women's ministries—one that prioritizes spiritual exploration, emotional authenticity, and leadership development for women. Only by expanding beyond the narrow confines of submission and service can these institutions hope to reconnect with the women they risk losing.

Psychological Autonomy and the Path to Self-Governance

Reclaiming self-governance is not just about freeing ourselves from external control. It's also about reclaiming the internal capacity to make decisions that are right for us. Psychological autonomy is the foundation of this process—having the freedom and the internal resources to think for ourselves, act in alignment with our values, and trust our emotions and instincts.

Psychological autonomy means developing the ability to guide your own behavior, thoughts, and feelings in ways that honor your internal compass, not external pressures.[9]

For many women, this ability has been slowly eroded over time. Patriarchal conditioning teaches us to distrust our own desires and decisions, making us reliant on outside authority figures, whether they be husbands, pastors, or societal norms.

Reclaiming psychological autonomy is about unlearning those habits and instead developing the confidence to trust your own judgment without constantly seeking validation from others. When you start to listen to your inner voice, you begin to experience what true self-governance feels like—a state where you can confidently stand by your choices because they come from a place of authenticity and alignment with who you really are. This kind of self-governance echoes the wisdom and autonomy of the old witch in the woods—a powerful figure of independence and self-trust feared by patriarchal structures.

When you've been taught that men's authority over you is for your own good, it can feel disorienting to step into a space where you are the authority of your own life. Reclaiming your autonomy might initially feel like a rejection of the very protection you've been told you need, but it's important to see this "protection" for what it really is—control. And once you recognize that, the next step is building your own safety, confidence, and support network so you can step fully into your own authority without needing to rely on patriarchal systems for validation.

Autonomy versus Individualism: Finding Balance in Community

Reclaiming autonomy is often misinterpreted as a call to rugged individualism—a rejection of any connection, care, or dependence on others. But true autonomy is not about isolation; it's about the freedom to choose how you engage with the world while maintaining deep, mutual connections with others. Autonomy thrives in spaces where relationships are built on respect, equality, and interdependence rather than control or obligation.

It's important to recognize that autonomy and communal connection are not opposites—they're complementary. Autonomy allows you to show up as your whole self in relationships, offering care and receiving it without losing your sense of self. In contrast, patriarchal systems often teach women that "goodness" means self-sacrifice to the point of erasure. This dynamic leaves women disconnected not only from themselves but also from the true, life-giving potential of communal bonds.

Friendships, family ties, and broader community networks can be powerful tools for autonomy when approached with mutual respect. A community rooted in mutual care acknowledges that everyone—yourself included—has value, wisdom, and unique contributions. This contrasts sharply with relationships shaped by patriarchal norms, where care is one-sided and often transactional, leaving women feeling depleted and unseen.

For example, consider friendships that encourage you to embrace your whole emotional and intellectual self. In these spaces, autonomy is not compromised by sharing your struggles or leaning on others for support. Instead, your autonomy is reinforced by the understanding that you can be fully known and accepted without having to perform or conform. Research shows that supportive relationships are vital for emotional well-being and resilience, and they often foster a deeper sense of autonomy by reinforcing self-worth and validation of your own voice.[10]

In communal spaces, autonomy is also about giving as much as it is about receiving. While patriarchy often casts care and connection as inherently sacrificial for women, mutual relationships allow us to reframe care as something enriching rather than depleting. For example, in mutual partnerships or community settings, autonomy is expressed when care flows both ways: you can support others without losing yourself and also allow others to care for you without feeling "weak" or dependent.

This dynamic is particularly crucial in broader communal ties. Whether through shared causes, spiritual spaces, or neighborhood networks, autonomy can coexist with collaboration. In fact, true autonomy flourishes in community spaces where everyone is seen and valued for who they are, rather than their ability to conform to patriarchal ideals. For many women, reclaiming autonomy also means finding or building these spaces where care and connection are mutual and nourishing.

Ultimately, autonomy is about choice—the choice to care, to connect, and to rely on others while staying deeply rooted in yourself. It's about rejecting the binary that says you must either be independent and self-sufficient or dependent and subordinate. By stepping into relationships as a whole, autonomous person, you create bonds that empower both yourself and those around you, allowing everyone to flourish together.

Autonomy and Social Relationships

It's important to understand that reclaiming self-governance doesn't mean rejecting all forms of authority. In our world, hierarchies exist—whether in work, family, or community spaces—and we still have to interact with them. But the difference lies in how we approach these hierarchies. Research shows that autonomy and healthy relationships are not mutually exclusive. In fact, psychological autonomy allows us to engage with others in ways that are respectful and empowering without sacrificing our own voice.[11]

What's crucial is that you don't feel obligated to submit simply because an authority figure—especially a male one—tells you to. This doesn't mean rejecting all hierarchies, but it does mean discerning when authority is healthy and when it's oppressive. True autonomy is about discerning when a hierarchy is based on mutual respect and when it's simply a mechanism for enforcing control. Healthy hierarchies allow space for collaboration, shared decision-making, and respect for all voices.

Toxic hierarchies demand absolute submission to male headship, especially males with power in the Christian patriarchal system. Patriarchal relationships thrive when women are isolated from themselves and each other, disconnected from both internal wisdom and potential support. The key is knowing the difference and, more importantly, trusting yourself to navigate these spaces without surrendering your autonomy. Self-governance means walking into every room, knowing you are your own authority.

By rejecting the way Christian patriarchy has vilified what your inner wisdom knows to be true, you begin to know intuitively what you want and what is going to lead you to flourishing. You have the right to decide which voices you listen to and which you reject.

When you step into a room—whether at work, in a family setting, or in a social context—recognize that your wisdom is valid. You do not need to defer to anyone simply because of their title or gender. You are capable of discerning when it's appropriate to follow guidance and when it's necessary to stand firm in your autonomy. This approach allows you to navigate power dynamics without surrendering your self-governance.

The Benefits of Reclaiming Self-Governance

Reclaiming self-governance offers women a profound sense of freedom and empowerment. Emotionally and psychologically, women who reclaim their autonomy report a stronger sense of self-worth and confidence in their decision-making abilities. They no longer rely on male figures for validation or approval, trusting instead in their own wisdom.

Women who leave oppressive religious environments often describe feeling liberated, able to make choices that align with their values and desires without fear of judgment. For instance, in her memoir *Out of Faith*, Maria Compton recounts her story of liberation from the restrictive Plymouth Brethren Christian Church.[12] In her post-fundamentalist life, she celebrates flourishing and exploring simple expressions of her personality that were formerly off-limits, like jewelry, fun clothes, and changing her hair color.[13]

Her narrative, and those of many others sharing their stories online, in books, and through documentaries, underscores the profound sense of empowerment and self-determination that many women report after departing from restrictive religious settings.

Physically, reclaiming bodily autonomy leads to better health outcomes. Reclaiming autonomy in various aspects of life, beyond healthcare decisions, significantly enhances women's overall well-being. Autonomy empowers women to make choices aligned with their values and aspirations, leading to improved mental health, increased self-efficacy, and greater life satisfaction. For instance, a study published in BMC Public Health found that higher self-efficacy—a component of personal autonomy—is associated with more autonomous decision-making among women, which in turn positively influences their health and nutrition outcomes.[14] This data underscores the importance of fostering autonomy not only in healthcare but across all domains of life to promote holistic well-being for women.

Women who have access to birth control, safe abortions, and healthcare that honors their choices experience improved physical and mental well-being.[15] Rejecting the shame of purity culture allows women to develop healthier relationships with their bodies and sexuality. Women are no longer constrained by patriarchal teachings that tie their worth to their virginity or their role as mothers. Instead, they embrace a holistic understanding of their bodies as sacred, autonomous, and worthy of both care and pleasure.

In relationships, reclaiming self-governance allows women to enter partnerships rooted in mutual respect and shared decision-making. Studies show that shared decision-making in relationships leads to greater satisfaction for both partners.[16] These relationships are built on trust and collaboration, not control or submission. Both partners' needs are honored, creating healthier, more fulfilling dynamics.

Spiritually, women who govern their own spiritual lives find deeper connections to the Divine. Whether through intuitive practices, expansive reading lists, or earth-based rituals, these women explore spiritual paths that honor their feminine wisdom. They are no longer confined to male-dominated religious structures but instead find meaning in practices that affirm their autonomy and spiritual authority.

Learning to Choose Your Own Path

The process of reclaiming self-governance begins with recognizing where patriarchal conditioning still holds sway in your life. These beliefs often show up in subtle ways—self-doubt, hesitancy to speak up, or a need for validation before making decisions.

Journaling can be a helpful tool for identifying these patterns. Set aside time each day to reflect on decisions you've made, conversations you've had, or feelings that have surfaced. Ask yourself, "Did I approach this situation from a place of autonomy, or was I seeking approval or permission?" Over time, this practice will help you untangle patriarchal conditioning from your sense of self.

Reconnecting with your own wisdom is key to reclaiming autonomy. Patriarchal systems have long taught women to suppress their gut instincts and bodily responses, but these internal signals are essential to self-governance. Start by trusting what feels right to you, whether in daily routines, spiritual practices, or personal boundaries.

Establishing boundaries in relationships is an important part of this process. Women who have been conditioned to submit to male authority may struggle with setting boundaries, especially in relationships. It's important to communicate your needs and desires clearly and to discern which relationships are safe to share your deeper, more intimate self. Not everyone will be safe enough to discuss your spiritual journey or your bodily autonomy. Take time to assess which people in your life respect your autonomy and wisdom before opening up to them.

Healing your shame around autonomy is also crucial. Women who have been denied self-governance often feel guilty or selfish when they begin reclaiming their power. Practice self-compassion as you navigate these feelings. Remind yourself that autonomy is not selfish; it's the birthright of every human being, including you. Use affirmations or mindfulness techniques to replace negative thoughts with compassion and affirm your right to govern your own life.

Embodied Self-Governance: Moving Wisdom into the Body

By now, you've hopefully begun to untangle your body from the toxic grip of Christian patriarchy. You've recognized how this system has separated you from your physical self, made you distrust your body's wisdom, and imposed layers of guilt and shame over natural desires and instincts. Reclaiming self-governance isn't just an intellectual exercise—it's a deeply embodied practice. It's about reclaiming your body as a source of wisdom and letting that wisdom guide you in reconnecting with your full self.

Embodied self-governance means learning to inhabit your body fully, allowing her to be your partner in the decisions you make, rather than a vessel controlled by external forces. When you engage in self-governance from an embodied place, you're not just *thinking* about what feels right—you're *actually feeling* it. You're tuning into the sensations that tell you when something aligns with your inner knowing or when it feels out of balance.

Movement can be a powerful tool in this process. Whether it's through yoga, dance, walking, or even just stretching, find ways to move your body that make you feel alive, grounded, and connected to your wisdom. Movement helps you break free from the mind–body divide that patriarchal teachings often enforce, reminding you that your body is an integral part of your decision-making process.

Consider integrating daily practices that invite your body to speak—such as setting aside time for deep breathing, meditating on the sensations in your body, or engaging in intuitive movement where you let your body guide you. As you move, ask yourself questions like, "What does my body need right now?" and "How can I honor my body's wisdom today?"

The answers to these questions will help you build a more holistic form of self-governance that honors the wisdom of your body as much as that of your mind and spirit.

Affirming and Protecting Your Space for Growth

Reclaiming your autonomy isn't just about taking control of your decisions—it's also about proactively making space for yourself in a world that constantly assumes women should do more and be more for everyone else. Let's be honest: Tasks like planning events, cooking, cleaning, laundry, scheduling appointments, and even decorating often land on women's shoulders without anyone even talking about it. It's just expected.

A 2021 Pew Research Center study showed that in opposite-sex partnerships, nearly 60 percent of women said they handle more of the housework than their partners, while only 6 percent of men agreed their partners do more. Mothers, in particular, take on the mental load of managing kids' schedules, with 74 percent saying they do more than their male partners.[17]

It's no wonder so many of us feel stretched thin. Even as society progresses in other areas, a lot of this invisible work still falls to women. A 2024 article in *The Atlantic* pointed out that despite cultural shifts, women are still taking on the majority of household chores and emotional labor, whether or not they work outside the home. This imbalance not only adds stress but can also leave you feeling unseen and undervalued.[18]

So, how do we start protecting our time and energy without feeling guilty? It begins with setting boundaries that honor your needs. Take a look at all the things you're doing and ask yourself: Which of these truly matter to me? Which ones are just being silently handed to me? Where you can, share the load, say no, or let go of what doesn't align with your values. Your time is just as valuable as anyone else's, and it's okay to prioritize yourself.

It's also important to create sacred, nonnegotiable time for yourself—a morning ritual, a daily walk, or a quiet hour in the evening that's all yours. Make it meaningful: Light a candle, journal, or create a small space in your home that feels peaceful and affirming. Surround yourself with reminders of why this time matters—a favorite book, a photo, or something symbolic of your journey.

Protecting this space isn't just about taking a break; it's about showing yourself and the world that your growth and well-being are important. It's about breaking the cycle of constantly being "on call" for everyone else's needs. When you protect your time and energy, you challenge the systems that expect you to carry the invisible load without question. You remind yourself—and everyone else—that your autonomy and your journey toward wholeness are worth it. By making this space, you create a foundation for your self-governance to thrive, free from interruptions or compromises. And that's not just self-care; it's reclaiming your power.

Leaning In: A Date with Your Younger Self

Plan a special date with your younger self—a day dedicated to doing exactly what the two of you want, free from obligations or expectations. This is about reconnecting with the part of you who once dreamed freely, before the world told you who to be, and celebrating the joy of making choices just for yourself.

Step 1: Connect with Your Younger Self

Take a few moments to imagine your younger self sitting across from you. Ask her what she dreams of doing, what she's curious about, or what has always brought her joy. This doesn't have to be grand—sometimes the simplest desires hold the most meaning.

Step 2: Plan Your Date

Choose an activity (or a few) that honors her preferences. Maybe it's something playful, like drawing, dancing, or eating your favorite childhood treat. Or perhaps it's visiting a place that feels peaceful, inspiring, or nostalgic. Let her guide you.

Focus on making choices that feel authentic and free—this day is about celebrating the beauty of doing what you love without judgment or expectation.

Step 3: Celebrate the Little Moments

As you spend time together, pay attention to the small moments that feel joyful, freeing, or meaningful. Notice how it feels to honor her preferences and allow yourself to simply be. These little moments of autonomy are worth celebrating. It's completely normal and healthy for grief to come up during these moments, especially if your younger self didn't have permission to experience these activities and feelings.

Step 4: Create or Collect Reminders of Your Time Together

At the end of your date, find a way to hold onto the experience. This could be:

- a keepsake from your day (a flower, a small object, or something symbolic);
- a journal entry about what you did, how it felt, and what you learned about yourself;
- a photo, drawing, or memento that captures the joy of your time together.

Keep this reminder somewhere you can easily see or touch it—your pocket, a desk, or your phone. When you find yourself in environments where you have less freedom, these reminders will help you reconnect with that sense of autonomy and self-celebration.

This date is more than just a fun activity—it's an act of reclaiming your voice, your joy, and your right to make choices for yourself. By honoring your younger self, you're affirming that her dreams and desires still matter, and that you have the power to carry her wisdom forward into your life today.

Chapter 8

Leading

From an early age, many women raised in Christian patriarchal culture are taught that our natural leadership abilities are "too much," "too assertive," "untrustworthy," and even "heretical." Whether through subtle societal messages or overt discouragement, the underlying message has often been that our voices don't belong at the front. This isn't a reflection of our abilities; it's rooted in Christian patriarchy's teachings about traditional male and female roles, which separate leadership and strength from what's often characterized as "feminine." These teachings don't simply discourage women—they foster inner doubts, pit us against our natural gifts, and create barriers to self-trust and authentic leadership.

But imagine a world where we feel as free to lead as we do to breathe, where we know in our bones that we're capable, wise, and fully equipped. Every time we feel a pull to guide, to make a decision, or to speak up, we are experiencing moments of our natural leadership. This chapter invites us to embrace those instincts, recognizing them as glimpses of our strength and capacity to lead, while also offering practical steps to expand our sense of leadership. Together, let's reclaim the wholeness of our leadership as an act of self-liberation and collective empowerment.

How Christian Patriarchy Diminishes Women's Leadership

The roots of the belief that women are unfit to lead are deeply embedded in Christian teachings. From the beginning, religious doctrine has been used to diminish women's roles in leadership, promoting the idea that women are inherently subordinate to men. For example, the story of Eve (again) is often interpreted to cast women as inherently untrustworthy and has reinforced the narrative that men must lead while women follow.

For centuries, Christian patriarchy has relied on snippets of Scripture to marginalize women's leadership, perpetuating the belief that women are inherently unfit to lead. One of the most commonly cited verses is 1 Timothy 2:12: "I do not permit a woman to teach or to assume authority over a man; she must be quiet." This verse has been used as a foundation to exclude women from pastoral and leadership roles in many Christian denominations, such as the Southern Baptist Convention[1] and Roman Catholic Church.[2]

As I discuss in my article, "Five Ways the Bible Supports Women Preaching,"[3] this interpretation of 1 Timothy 2:12 often relies on taking Scripture out of context. Paul's words in this passage were most likely directed at specific women in Timothy's church who were being disruptive, not all women across all times. The original Greek term *authentein*, often translated as "assume authority," more accurately means "to usurp or take authority illegitimately"—a principle that applies to both men and women.[4]

By isolating this single verse, patriarchal systems rewrite the broader biblical narrative that clearly demonstrates God's support for women in leadership. The Bible includes numerous examples of women leading both spiritually and politically. Deborah served as a judge and military leader over Israel (Judges 4–5). Phoebe was a deacon trusted by Paul to deliver and interpret his letter to the Romans (Romans 16:1–2). Priscilla co-led and taught with her husband in Ephesus (Acts 18:24–26). And Mary Magdalene was the first person commissioned by Jesus to proclaim his resurrection—a role that made her the first preacher of the gospel (John 20:16–18).[5] These examples highlight that leadership is not restricted by gender in God's design.[6]

Blocking women from top roles doesn't stop at religious institutions. It extends into our social, political, and business spaces, limiting women's voices and reinforcing the idea that we belong in supportive, not directive, roles. Patriarchal norms have traditionally assigned leadership to men in external, public-facing roles, while women are restricted to nurturing roles or placed under male headship in the family, workplace, or church. By upholding these "traditional" distinctions and assigning rigid roles that fail to honor the complexity of human qualities and strengths, we limit the full potential of all individuals. As a result, we diminish the diversity of strengths needed for vibrant, inclusive leadership and perpetuate a cycle where women continue to feel held back from stepping into their full potential.

Countering Misogyny with Archetypal Masculine and Feminine Qualities

In contrast to rigid "traditional" roles, archetypal masculine and feminine qualities represent universal human attributes that transcend gender. Archetypal masculine traits include assertiveness, clarity, structure, and action, while archetypal feminine qualities encompass empathy, intuition, relational intelligence, and collaboration. These qualities aren't exclusive to any gender but are energies we can all embody. When integrated, they create a balanced approach to leadership that respects the full range of human experience and potential without inflicting gender-based limitations.

The most impactful leaders are those who can harmonize masculine and feminine attributes within themselves. Leaders who balance assertiveness with empathy, structure with relational awareness, and clarity with intuition are better able to motivate people without causing fear or exploitation. These leaders inspire trust, resilience, and engagement by encouraging authentic expression and fostering a shared sense of purpose.

Society often labels rigid roles as "traditional" to suggest they're natural or beneficial, but these roles are rooted not in nature but in centuries of patriarchal structures that constrain people's potential based on gender. Rather than reflecting inherent human capacities, these restrictive roles distort our understanding of both masculinity and femininity, boxing us into narrow definitions. In a more integrated model of leadership, we're encouraged to embody a blend of qualities based on the needs of the moment and our unique strengths. In doing so, we foster resilient, inclusive environments where everyone can thrive without feeling confined by stereotypes or outdated expectations.

I'm going to say something that may seem controversial, especially if taken out of context, but in some ways, misogynists aren't entirely wrong when they point to women's struggles with leadership. But it's not for the reasons they claim. There's a smoke-and-mirrors act here, where Christian patriarchy casts blame on our inherent nature or suggests that God created us "unfit" to lead. The truth is, it's the systematized stripping away of our inner truth and full spectrum of attributes that leaves us doubting our capacity to lead with confidence and impact.

In earlier chapters, we explored the value of empathy, intuition, and emotional insight—qualities deeply connected to our sense of self and our connections with others. Yet, these very traits are often weaponized against us in leadership contexts. Under the framework of Christian patriarchy, empathy becomes "emotional fragility," intuition is dismissed as "unreliable," and relational intelligence is trivialized as "soft"—all framing us as unsuited to lead and reinforcing the idea that our place is in service, not leadership. This narrative pits us against our gifts, making us question our own worthiness to lead rather than celebrating the unique strengths we bring to any role.

When we internalize these teachings, they become the lens through which we view ourselves, eroding our confidence and stifling our natural gifts. Entering the real world, we carry these doubts, and every stumble or hesitation reinforces the idea that we aren't fit to lead. This internal conflict creates a cycle of self-questioning, making authentic leadership feel out of reach—a struggle compounded by other women who, lacking self-awareness, unconsciously reinforce these same oppressive beliefs. Instead of solidarity, we often encounter judgment from within, as the cycle of undermining continues, now enforced by our own peers. Misogyny and disembodiment run rampant, affecting everyone. This isn't limited to women or femme-presenting Queer individuals; men, too, who are conditioned to "man up" and dismiss archetypal feminine strengths as weaknesses, are cut off from leading from a whole, healed place, leaving us all to pay the price.

The Internalization of Patriarchal Narratives

One of the most damaging aspects of Christian patriarchy is how deeply it conditions women to internalize harmful beliefs about their unfitness to lead. This conditioning isn't merely a social influence; it's the product of lifelong exposure to systems that link our worth with submission, purity, and beauty. As these beliefs settle in, they shape our perception of ourselves and others, often making us unwitting gatekeepers of patriarchal norms, where conformity feels safer than stepping into our power.

For instance, women raised in patriarchal teachings may come to associate authority and autonomy with men, disconnecting us from our inner wisdom. This phenomenon is sometimes called "pink patriarchy," where women uphold values that restrict their own and other women's roles. Figures like Phyllis Schlafly, the politically conservative social crusader who opposed the Equal Rights Amendment in the 1970s, exemplify this dynamic. Schlafly's public career was based on her advocacy for "traditional gender roles" and vehemently opposing the Equal Rights Amendment, even though her success itself contradicted her claims. While proudly describing herself as a wife and homemaker, Schlafly was a political activist, leader of the anti-feminism movement, and even earned a law degree in 1978, all while her school-age children and home were cared for by "domestic help."[7]

Today, TERFs (Trans-Exclusionary Radical Feminists) similarly reinforce patriarchal control by limiting the definition of "woman" to Christian patriarchal standards, excluding trans women and constraining feminism's potential to challenge oppressive systems. Feminism at its heart is gender equity work, but excluding and vilifying trans women reinforces patriarchal gender definitions. Trans women typically face the same (but more severe) struggles as cisgender women—violence, discrimination, and societal expectations rooted in patriarchy—yet they're often pushed out of spaces that should protect and cherish them.[8] This exclusion doesn't just harm trans people; it weakens feminism itself by dividing a movement that thrives on unity and inclusion. If we want to challenge the systems that hold us all back, we need to embrace and support everyone fighting alongside us, recognizing that our differences make us stronger, not weaker. Feminism should be a space of hope, belonging, and action for all who strive for equality.

The cycle of enforcing and perpetuating patriarchal values can become even more entrenched when women encounter others who embody a balanced, integrated expression of leadership. A woman grounded in her wisdom and confidence can feel threatening to those still clinging to limiting beliefs.

Instead of being inspired, some respond by tearing down the embodied woman, reinforcing the false notion that power is limited. Breaking free from these harmful narratives requires us to question where we've internalized limitations and reclaim our power, supporting each other rather than allowing patriarchal norms to divide us.

Healing Our Way Out of Patriarchy

The pink patriarchy is rooted in deep-seated fear and insecurity. Many women feel unsafe stepping outside these prescribed roles because our identities and self-worth have become intricately tied to patriarchal standards. For those who've been deeply wounded by these teachings, the prospect of change—especially change that empowers other women—can feel destabilizing. Instead of finding solidarity, some women may lash out, clinging to the structures they believe provide security.

These reactions are often responses to unresolved trauma. Patriarchal systems thrive on pitting women against each other, fostering competition instead of collaboration. Healing from this conditioning requires confronting how we may have contributed to our own oppression and choosing a path forward that includes mutual support and empathy. Reclaiming leadership from this space of healing opens new possibilities for everyone, creating a culture of leadership grounded in wholeness and balance rather than fear and restriction.

Leaning In: Stepping Out of the Shadows

Validate your existing skills: Recognize the leadership you already bring into your life, whether managing responsibilities, supporting friends, or leading a project. Keep a journal to remind yourself of your inherent strengths.

Trust your intuition and empathy: Embrace your intuition and empathy as valuable tools. Begin by trusting your instincts in small decisions, noticing how self-trust builds over time.

Find a supportive community: Surround yourself with those who affirm your strengths and help you grow as a leader. Seek out communities that support balanced, authentic leadership.

Practice daily acts of self-trust: Each day, reinforce your inner authority by making a decision without consulting others or setting a meaningful boundary. Over time, this habit builds confidence in your leadership abilities.

Step 1: Where Is Your Leadership Honored?

Reflect on the areas of your life where your leadership is seen, valued, and celebrated. Ask yourself:

- In which relationships or communities do people express gratitude for how I show up?
- Where do I feel my efforts are making an impact?
- How does it feel to be recognized for my contributions?

Write down specific examples of moments or spaces where your leadership is appreciated.

Step 2: What's Your Superpower?

Identify the unique qualities that make your leadership effective and authentic. Reflect on these questions:

- What strengths do I bring to my leadership roles (e.g., empathy, creativity, organization)?
- How do these qualities influence the way I show up for myself and others?
- In what ways do my superpowers create positive change in my relationships and communities?

Celebrate the unique aspects of your leadership and consider how they contribute to the spaces where you lead.

Step 3: Where Is Your Leadership Overlooked?

Now think about the areas where your leadership may go unnoticed or unacknowledged. Consider:

- Are there relationships or situations where my efforts feel taken for granted?
- Do I find myself leading in ways that don't align with my values or bring me joy?
- Are there areas where I wish my contributions were more appreciated or respected?

Write down the situations where your leadership doesn't feel recognized or valued.

Step 4: Reflect on the Cost of Leading in Unappreciative or Unhealthy Spaces

Leading in spaces where your contributions are undervalued can take a toll. Reflect on these questions:

- What does it cost me emotionally, mentally, physically, or spiritually to lead in these areas?
- How does this impact my sense of self or my ability to lead effectively in other parts of my life?
- Are these costs sustainable, or do they require reevaluating my role in these spaces?

Take time to acknowledge how these experiences affect you and what boundaries or changes might be necessary.

Step 5: What Do You Want to Do with This Insight?

With these reflections in mind, think about how you want to move forward:

- Celebrate what feels good: How can you lean further into the spaces where your leadership is honored and fulfilling? What would it look like to prioritize these areas more often?
- Shift or release what doesn't serve you: Are there ways to set boundaries or step back from areas where your leadership isn't valued? What would it feel like to redirect your energy toward places that bring you joy and growth?

Write a short note to yourself about how you'd like to move forward, whether it's celebrating the areas where you feel valued or making changes to protect your energy.

Chapter 9

Wisdom

Many of us have been taught—directly and indirectly—that our wisdom and deep inner knowing are unreliable because we are women. We've been encouraged to question our instincts, to seek out "expert" advice over the subtle nudges from within. This disconnect isn't a coincidence but rather a result of Christian patriarchal teachings that promote the idea that authority and wisdom come from outside of ourselves—from rigid doctrines or the voices of those traditionally in power. By teaching us to doubt ourselves, these systems create and reinforce our dependence on external validation and diminish the very qualities that enable us to know and trust our own truths. Imagine the strength and autonomy that could be gained if we truly believed our wisdom was just as valuable as any "official" knowledge.

Imagine the power of embracing all aspects of wisdom—a holistic approach that values inner wisdom, experiential knowledge, professional insight, and academic study equally. When we honor each of these ways of knowing, we resist the restrictive, patriarchal notion that only formal education and structured knowledge are reliable. Recognizing all aspects of wisdom restores balance, giving us the autonomy to integrate our intuition, life experiences, professional insights, and learned knowledge as equally essential parts of who we are.

Reclaiming this inner knowing doesn't negate the value of formal education or structured knowledge but instead restores balance, reminding us that personal insight and lived experience hold inherent worth. When we are encouraged to honor this wisdom, we become empowered not just individually but collectively, gaining strength and resilience through our connection to ourselves and to each other. As we've already explored in chapters on embodiment, mothering, and autonomy, Christian patriarchy has a vested interest in keeping us disconnected from the full spectrum of our humanity. By severing us from our inner wisdom, the system ensures we remain disempowered and cut off from a deeper understanding of our own needs, potential, and purpose. But reconnecting with this inner voice offers a path back to ourselves, to our bodies, and to a more grounded, holistic way of being.

Think of all the times you've felt or sensed something to be true, even without "logical" evidence. Those moments are expressions of inner wisdom, often nudging us toward choices that align with our true selves. By learning to trust that inner guidance, we're able to resist the patterns of separation, reclaim our innate power, and ultimately build flourishing lives where we feel whole and connected.

Christian Patriarchy's Role in Dismissing Wisdom

Patriarchy has long controlled what knowledge is seen as valuable. It prioritizes technical, academic, and financial expertise—fields where men have historically dominated—while dismissing relational, emotional, and intuitive wisdom, often the domains of women and nonbinary individuals.

For instance, emotional intelligence and caregiving are seen as "natural" for women—something they inherently know how to do rather than as skills honed over years of practice. This assumption diminishes the true value of these contributions. Women are expected to shoulder emotional labor without recognition or compensation, and as they age, this work becomes even more invisible.

We see this dismissal play out in how society views leadership roles. While older men may be seen as wise and experienced leaders, older women are often considered out of touch or irrelevant. The patriarchal system celebrates aging men while marginalizing aging women.

Rediscovering Inner Wisdom: What It Means and Why It's Essential

Inner wisdom is our capacity to know, sense, and intuit truth without needing external validation. This knowledge is often emotional, relational, or embodied rather than strictly rational. It's the voice within that guides us toward compassion, empathy, and resilience—qualities frequently undervalued by frameworks that prioritize male authority and structured knowledge over the wisdom found in everyday experiences and embodied knowing. But such a viewpoint, which is often promoted in patriarchal Christian frameworks, isn't actually biblical or consistent with church tradition.

Both the Roman Catholic and Orthodox Christian traditions refer to divine wisdom in a personified female form called "Sophía," a direct translation from the Greek word *sophía*, meaning "wisdom" or "intelligence." This figure is often interpreted as the Holy Spirit—the third branch of the Trinity which is equal alongside the slightly more concrete images of God and Jesus. Sophía is the element of God within us who directs our conscience and our understanding. Sophía is a "she" rather than an "it"; she *is wisdom itself.* This is not a new concept. The word *sophia*, a feminine noun, appears 25 times in the New Testament,[1] and the famous Hagía Sophía church in Istanbul, which was constructed in the mid-sixth century CE, is named in honor of this figure.

Many of the earliest Christians understood that inner wisdom is a divine, praiseworthy, and particularly feminine attribute that is deeply tied to how we understand and move through the world. Sophía wisdom is inherently relational, often emerging from life experiences, empathy, and intuition.

But Christian patriarchy, at least in the West, has largely erased this tradition and instead teaches us to see these ways of knowing as untrustworthy, urging us to depend on religious or social authorities rather than our own experiences. By portraying women's innate and learned wisdom as unreliable, patriarchal structures reinforce a hierarchy where male authority figures are seen as the ultimate sources of guidance. This narrative is embedded in cultural, religious, and educational messages that frame emotional intelligence, relational insights, and embodied knowing as "lesser" ways of understanding. Over time, this erodes our trust in our inner compass, positioning ourselves as constantly in need of outside intervention and oversight, even in personal and private matters.

What's essential about inner wisdom is that it's ours—it emerges from within and aligns us with our values, helping us make choices that are true to who we are. Imagine living in a world where your inner knowing was honored just as much as any external measure of success. Imagine the strength of making decisions rooted in your sense of truth, free from the fear of judgment or the need for outside validation. Reclaiming this wisdom—*sophía*—is a return to yourself, connecting you to a deeper, more integrated way of living that is inherently resistant to patriarchal control. This is wisdom that lives in our bones, often cultivated in moments of quiet introspection, relational trust, and the freedom to explore our truest selves without pressure to perform or prove anything. Embracing inner wisdom allows us to break free from cycles of insecurity, grounding us in a truth that isn't tied to external validation but rooted in our connection to self and to others.

The disconnect from our inner wisdom isn't accidental; it's part of a larger system designed to keep us separate from our power. Christian patriarchy often teaches that wisdom is external, accessible only through religious leaders, doctrine, or institutional authority. This conditioning encourages women to dismiss their instincts, question their emotions, and rely on male authority figures—pastors, husbands, or fathers—for guidance. Women's ways of knowing—intuition, emotional depth, and relational intelligence—are often dismissed as secondary or unreliable.

In many patriarchal churches, Proverbs 3:5—"Trust in the Lord with all your heart and lean not on your own understanding"—is interpreted to discourage women from trusting their thoughts and intuition. These teachings suggest that relying on one's own understanding is dangerous, leading to the suppression of feminine wisdom and reinforcing male authority.[2] Women are often taught that trusting in God means deferring to male leaders for decisions, implying that their insights are insufficient.[3]

This perspective fosters dependence on male leadership. For example, in marital counseling, women might be told to "trust God" by submitting to their husbands' decisions, even when those decisions are harmful, framing submission as an act of faith.[4] When women challenge authority or raise concerns about unjust systems, Proverbs 3:5 is sometimes cited to silence them, suggesting that questioning authority equates to distrusting God.

For women called to leadership, these interpretations are particularly disheartening. Many are told that trusting God requires accepting male headship, limiting their ability to use their spiritual gifts. By creating an environment where women are expected to rely on external authority instead of their spiritual insights, these teachings uphold systems that prioritize male perspectives and suppress women's voices.

This separation from our inborn wisdom leads to inner conflict, creating a sense that our instincts are wrong or unworthy of trust. Over time, this disconnection leaves us fragmented, seeking external validation rather than cultivating trust in ourselves. It mirrors other forms of separation we've discussed: from our bodies, emotions, and nurturing instincts. Each layer compounds the last, keeping women disempowered and reliant on systems that benefit from this disconnection.

Yet Proverbs 3:5 does not require us to distrust ourselves. Instead, it encourages a partnership with God in decision-making—one that honors our intuition as a sacred gift. Embracing our inner wisdom can be a profound expression of faith.

Reconnecting with our inner wisdom is a healing journey. It restores autonomy, aligns us with our true selves, and challenges the disempowering narratives of Christian patriarchy. Trusting our intuition is a radical act—one that dissolves the lie that our knowledge is inadequate. It's a path to self-liberation that doesn't require anyone else's approval and leads us to the integrated, empowered selves we've always been.

On a spiritual level, the loss is even more profound. In many Indigenous and matriarchal societies, women are the keepers of spiritual traditions, maintaining the rituals, stories, and practices that connect the community to its roots and sense of belonging. These traditions are not just relics of the past but living practices that offer meaning, guidance, and purpose to the community. For example, in many Native American tribes, elder women play a central role in passing down oral histories, leading ceremonies, and teaching younger generations about their cultural heritage. Similarly, in matrilineal societies like the Minangkabau in Indonesia, women are deeply involved in preserving spiritual and communal practices, emphasizing the collective over the individual.

When these spiritual practices are lost, we risk becoming disconnected from our heritage, adrift in a world that prioritizes the material over the spiritual and the individual over the collective. The resulting spiritual disconnection often manifests as aimlessness or emptiness—a feeling of being unmoored from something greater than ourselves.

It's worth noting that these cultures often hold older women in high regard, valuing them as essential to the community's spiritual continuity. Unlike patriarchal systems, which tend to devalue women as they age, these societies view older women as repositories of wisdom and guardians of tradition. This unique perspective on aging affirms women's worth at every stage of life, which we'll explore further in the next section. Recognizing the importance of these traditions can inspire us to reclaim practices that connect us to our own sense of belonging and purpose, restoring the balance between the material and spiritual, the individual and collective.

The Personal Cost of Ignoring Inner Wisdom

Ignoring our inner wisdom comes at a high price, both emotionally and psychologically. When we're taught to distrust our instincts, self-doubt becomes a natural response. We second-guess our decisions, feel disconnected from ourselves, and are left in a constant state of uncertainty. This inner doubt echoes the disconnection we discussed in the chapter on autonomy, where relinquishing our sense of self leads to hesitation and confusion. Ignoring our inner wisdom leads to feelings of fragmentation, as if we're missing something essential within ourselves. Over time, this creates an emotional dissonance—a lingering sense that we're not fully present or aligned with who we truly are.

The consequences ripple outward. When we ignore our inner knowing, we may find ourselves in relationships, jobs, or situations that don't resonate with our values. We're more likely to stay in spaces that don't support our growth, all because we've been conditioned to believe that our own insights aren't enough. It's as though we're living out scripts written by someone else, making choices that don't truly reflect our own needs or desires. This perpetual state of compromise dulls our inner voice, making it harder to discern our true feelings and wishes. The longer we remain disconnected, the deeper the personal cost, eroding our trust in our own experience, leading us further from the people we were meant to become.

Reclaiming inner wisdom is, in many ways, reclaiming our true selves. It's a return to the wholeness that patriarchal systems have worked so hard to break apart. As we learn to honor our inner knowing, we begin to align more fully with who we are, allowing us to make choices that feel authentic and deeply nourishing. We start to break down the walls of isolation, forming a deeper connection to ourselves that extends to every relationship and decision we make. This reconnection is more than personal healing; it's an active resistance against the systems that sought to keep us small. By stepping into the fullness of our wisdom, we reclaim our lives in ways that support our deepest truths and honor our most essential selves.

The Societal Cost: When Women's Wisdom Is Silenced

The silencing of women's wisdom affects not only individuals but society as a whole. Christian patriarchy's focus on external authority devalues the qualities often associated with feminine wisdom—empathy, intuition, emotional insight, and relational intelligence. By suppressing these qualities, patriarchal systems limit the types of solutions and approaches that can address societal issues. For example, empathy and relational thinking are critical for healthcare, education, and environmental sustainability, but these qualities are often disregarded as "soft" or secondary in patriarchal cultures.

Imagine a world where feminine wisdom—intuitive knowing, emotional insight, and community-centered perspectives—was honored as *central* to societal health. We'd approach challenges from a more interconnected standpoint, valuing well-being and balance over profit and power. The systems we rely on, from healthcare to governance, would look drastically different, with a focus on collective flourishing rather than individual gain. The cost of ignoring these qualities is immense: We lose out on diverse solutions, compassionate policies, and a holistic approach to societal challenges that would benefit everyone. Honoring women's wisdom would mean inviting a new perspective into the public sphere—one that values interconnectedness and respects the wisdom that comes from life experiences, relationships, and empathy.

When women's wisdom is devalued, society is deprived of essential perspectives that could drive progress. Honoring inner wisdom isn't just a personal journey; it's a way to transform the world. By valuing diverse ways of knowing, we can move toward a future where connection, empathy, and balance are seen as strengths, not weaknesses. Imagine systems built on trust, respect, and collaboration—values that are often second nature to us. These systems would prioritize inclusivity, creating spaces where everyone's voice is heard, valued, and respected. In such a society, the wisdom of every person is seen as part of the collective strength, a foundation that allows us to thrive together.

Reclaiming Inner Wisdom in Our Daily Lives: What It Could Look Like

Imagine how life would change if you consistently trusted your inner wisdom. At an individual level, this might mean making choices based on what feels true to you, rather than what aligns with societal expectations. Imagine waking up each day and trusting that what you feel and sense is valid, that your intuition is a powerful guide. This level of self-trust allows us to move away from patterns of self-doubt and hesitation, making space for clarity, confidence, and joy. With every step we take grounded in our own wisdom, we're able to walk paths that feel purposeful and aligned with our core values.

In relationships, trusting our wisdom means we can communicate more authentically, set boundaries that feel right, and cultivate connections that support who we are. Trusting our wisdom is about showing up fully, knowing that our insights, needs, and boundaries are valid. When we bring this wisdom to our relationships, we foster spaces of mutual respect and understanding, where each person's truth is honored. This mirrors the themes of autonomy and self-nourishing, as we learn to prioritize our needs and truths in every interaction. Relationships grounded in shared respect and inner wisdom have the potential to deepen intimacy, build trust, and create spaces where vulnerability is met with compassion and authenticity.

On a larger scale, envisioning a society that values inner wisdom could lead to a more compassionate and sustainable world. When we reclaim our wisdom, we challenge patriarchal values that prioritize profit and power over empathy and balance. This shift has the potential to create a world where all ways of knowing are honored, making space for diverse solutions rooted in connection, care, and sustainability. A society that values wisdom from all aspects of life would honor the perspectives that come from experience, creating a balanced and harmonious world that recognizes the richness of every human experience. Together, we'd create environments where every person's truth adds to the collective strength, fostering communities where true understanding and lasting change are possible.

Practical Steps to Trust Your Inner Wisdom Again

Rebuilding trust in your inner wisdom doesn't have to involve grand gestures; it's about cultivating small, intentional practices. Begin each day with a check-in, asking, "What do I feel or sense today?" This practice allows space for your intuition to surface without interference from external influences. Reinforcing this with affirmations like "I trust my intuition" or "My inner wisdom is enough" can counteract self-doubt, especially when Christian patriarchy's messages of inadequacy start to creep in. Each affirmation strengthens our belief in our inner wisdom, gradually rewriting the narratives that conditioned us to feel inadequate.

Listening to your body is another crucial step. Our physical sensations often signal truths we might not yet realize mentally. Notice where you feel tension, warmth, or lightness, and let these cues inform your decisions. These sensations are reminders that wisdom lives within, in the form of embodied knowledge that guides us toward what's right for us. This body awareness becomes a valuable tool, helping us discern choices that align with our inner truths, fostering a sense of grounding and trust.

As you practice self-trust, consider letting go of the need for outside validation. While it can feel reassuring, external validation often detracts from our own sense of authority. By grounding yourself in your own wisdom, you'll find that your inner voice becomes a reliable source of strength and clarity. Gradually, you begin to discern when validation is helpful and when it holds you back from cultivating a deeper connection to yourself. The more we practice trusting our inner wisdom, the more we create lives that feel honest, grounded, and aligned with who we truly are.

Embracing Inner Wisdom as a Path to Personal and Collective Freedom

Reclaiming and trusting our inner wisdom is not just a personal journey but a revolutionary act against Christian patriarchy and its need for control. Each woman who reconnects with her inner knowing becomes part of a larger movement, challenging systems that rely on disconnection and hierarchy. By embracing this wisdom, we are collectively dismantling the structures that thrive on our self-doubt and separation from self.

Each choice to trust our inner wisdom strengthens this movement. In a world where feminine wisdom is valued, the impact would be felt in every part of society—from how we lead to how we build community. This is not about rejecting structured knowledge; it's about making room for *all* ways of knowing. Reclaiming our inner wisdom is both an act of personal empowerment and a step toward collective liberation. It's a path that values empathy, connection, and balance, fostering a world rooted in compassion and communal well-being. Together, we can forge new paths built on trust, respect, and a holistic understanding of the human experience, inviting in a future where everyone's wisdom is welcomed, honored, and celebrated.

The cost of being separated from our inner wisdom goes far beyond self-doubt or insecurity; it strikes at the core of our self-trust and spiritual identity. Growing up with the teachings of Christian patriarchy, we learned, directly or indirectly, that as women, our nature was inherently flawed and untrustworthy. We were taught that women are prone to deception, more likely to lead others astray, and in need of correction. We were taught to view our thoughts, instincts, even our bodies with suspicion, as if they might betray us at any moment. Our wisdom—the very instincts that make us who we are—was somehow considered dangerous or sinful. It was seen as something that needed guidance from external authorities to be "corrected."

Living with this narrative leaves a powerful, lingering sense of shame around our own inner knowing. When we're constantly told that our instincts, our emotions, and our bodies are somehow flawed, then trusting ourselves feels like an act of rebellion. The message wasn't just that our instincts might be misguided but that our deepest impulses were tainted by an innate tendency toward error. Spiritually, this teaching has cut us off from a direct connection to ourselves and to the Divine. Instead of feeling that we have a right to access wisdom or guidance directly from within (*sophía*) we were taught to look outward for validation—to rely on religious authorities or established doctrines, as if wisdom and worth were only accessible through someone else's permission.

These teachings set up an inner conflict, making us second-guess ourselves, question our thoughts, and feel suspicious of our emotions. Even when we sensed something deeply, Christian patriarchy urged us to dismiss it, reinforcing the belief that wisdom had to come from outside. This doubt affects more than just our decisions; it isolates us from our own sense of spirituality. If we can't fully trust ourselves, how can we trust any divine connection we might feel? Every time we feel an intuitive nudge, we've been taught to check it against the external standards we were raised with, reinforcing the notion that our wisdom alone is somehow lacking or dangerous.

This conditioning isn't just emotionally painful; it's a kind of spiritual fragmentation that leaves us dependent on systems designed to keep us in doubt. Over time, we might start to recognize how much of our energy is spent second-guessing ourselves, apologizing for our instincts, and allowing others' voices to be louder than our own. We begin to see how Christian patriarchy encourages this doubt as a way to keep women spiritually disempowered, to make us feel that we need its approval to connect to the sacred or to trust ourselves fully.

Reclaiming our inner wisdom is, for us, a journey back to wholeness and self-trust. Every time we choose to believe in our insights, honor our instincts, or let our feelings guide us, we're actively breaking away from the narrative of inherent sinfulness we were raised with. Reclaiming this inner voice is a way of creating a direct connection to spirituality, one where we don't need anyone else's approval to feel whole, wise, or worthy. As we embrace our inner wisdom, we're rewriting what spirituality means, grounding it in our experiences and values and finally allowing ourselves to trust our own truth without apology.

Leaning In: Celebrating Your Wisdom

This activity is designed to help you recognize, honor, and celebrate the wisdom you already hold. It's not about striving for more or proving yourself—it's about pausing to acknowledge the depth of your knowledge and intuition and embracing it as enough, just as it is.

Step 1: Reflect on Your Wisdom

Take a moment to reflect on the ways your wisdom has shown up in your life. Ask yourself:

- When have I trusted my instincts and had them lead me to something good or true?
- What life experiences have taught me valuable lessons that I now carry with me?
- How have I shared my wisdom with others in ways that supported or encouraged them?

Write down at least three examples where your wisdom has guided you or positively impacted your life or others.

Step 2: Celebrate Your Unique Ways of Knowing

Think about how your wisdom expresses itself. Reflect on these questions:

- What forms does my wisdom take (e.g., intuition, empathy, creativity, practical knowledge, lived experiences)?

- What strengths do I bring to my decision-making or the way I navigate challenges?
- How does my wisdom feel when I trust it—calm, grounded, clear, powerful?

Write a short affirmation or description of what makes your wisdom unique and meaningful. For example, "My wisdom is rooted in my deep empathy and the care I show to others," or "My intuition has always been a quiet but powerful guide in my life."

Step 3: Anchor Your Wisdom

Create or choose something that symbolizes your wisdom and serves as a reminder of your inner knowing. It could be:

- a favorite quote or affirmation that resonates with your sense of wisdom;
- a small object, like a stone, piece of jewelry, or keepsake that feels grounding and significant;
- a journal entry or piece of art that captures the essence of your wisdom.

Keep this anchor somewhere you can see or hold it regularly. Use it as a touchpoint when you feel disconnected or doubtful, reminding yourself of the deep well of wisdom you already possess.

Step 4: Honor and Share Your Wisdom

Consider how you can honor your wisdom in your daily life. Ask yourself:

- How can I trust my inner knowing more fully in my decisions and interactions?

- Are there ways I'd like to share my wisdom—through mentoring, storytelling, or simply showing up authentically?
- How can I remind myself that my wisdom is enough, just as it is, without needing external validation?

Write a short commitment to yourself, celebrating the wisdom you hold and affirming how you'll honor it moving forward. For example: "I will trust my instincts and honor the lessons I've learned, knowing that my wisdom is a gift to myself and others."

Chapter 10

Aging

I don't need to tell you that society is obsessed with women's youth and perceived innocence. From skincare routines designed to erase normal wrinkles to media that glorifies the vitality of youth over the experience of age, it's no wonder that we've grown to fear the natural process of aging. Ageism, particularly for women and nonbinary individuals who present as female, often centers around the body—how we look, how our energy shifts, how our bodies change. But the impact of aging goes far beyond the physical. It touches our wisdom, our experience, and how society views our capacity to contribute.

In this chapter, we're going to move beyond the obsession with youthful appearances and delve into something far more important: the wisdom that can only come with age. Aging is a process that should be celebrated as it is a deepening of wisdom, but our culture tends to discard everything to do with it, including the very knowledge that comes with it. Particularly for women, aging becomes a process of fading into the background, even as we accumulate rich experiences that could benefit our communities.

Forced Irrelevance

In modern patriarchal society, the wisdom of older generations is often dismissed or outright ignored, especially when it comes from women and nonbinary individuals. Patriarchal and capitalist structures prioritize the economic productivity and youthful energy of individuals while devaluing the deep insights that come from a lifetime of experience. Older women, in particular, are pushed aside in favor of younger voices and bodies, even when they hold the expertise and emotional intelligence that younger generations desperately need.

Capitalist systems measure worth through productivity—how much one can contribute to the economy. This means that once people retire, especially those in professions like caregiving or emotional labor, society begins to view them as less valuable. For women and nonbinary individuals, who are often pushed into caregiving roles and informal labor by family members, this shift is even more pronounced. The experience they've gained is often tied to relational, emotional, or spiritual wisdom—qualities that are undervalued in a capitalist framework.

Consider the wisdom that comes with decades of caregiving, community-building, or spiritual development. This isn't the kind of knowledge you'll find in textbooks, but it's incredibly powerful. It's the ability to see long-term patterns in relationships, to know when someone needs a compassionate ear, to offer guidance that's rooted in lived experience. And yet, this type of wisdom is often dismissed as "soft skills" and seen as less important than the "hard skills" so highly valued for economic output or stemming from traditionally male-dominated spaces like academia, corporate offices, or the military.

When society pushes older women into the background, we lose access to this wisdom. We lose the relational expertise that could strengthen communities, the emotional intelligence that could help us navigate crises, and the spiritual insight that could guide us toward more fulfilling, balanced lives.

The Hypocrisy of How Aging Affects Men and Women Differently

Christian patriarchy has long driven an obsession with young, "pure" virgins, painting women as most valuable in their youth when untouched by sexual experience. This harmful narrative ties a woman's worth to her body and purity, setting an expiration date on her societal value. As women age, this value—rooted in patriarchal ideals—diminishes, while men are encouraged to grow into their power, intellect, and experience.

This double standard is pervasive across both Christian and secular cultures. In patriarchal Christianity, the emphasis on a woman's youth reinforces the belief that her greatest contributions are tied to physical beauty and reproductive potential. In secular spaces, such as Hollywood and the media, this obsession with youth takes a slightly different form but produces similar outcomes. Actresses, models, and public figures are often discarded as they age, while aging male counterparts are celebrated for their distinguished appearances, accomplishments, and continued sexual prowess.

We see the hypocrisy everywhere. Older male celebrities or public figures are often called "silver foxes," their gray hair and wrinkles framed as signs of wisdom and experience. Men are allowed to hold onto positions of power and influence, celebrated for their achievements and intellect, no matter their age. Women, however, are judged by a much harsher standard. They are often encouraged to hide signs of aging through anti-aging treatments or are pushed out of the public eye entirely. This societal disparity reflects a broader devaluation of women's aging process, framing it as a decline rather than a natural progression of insight and wisdom.

The problem isn't that women lose their value as they age—it's that society stops looking for it. Patriarchal frameworks, religious and secular alike, uphold the notion that youth is a woman's greatest asset, while age and experience are celebrated in men. This isn't about women losing wisdom or relevance as they grow older; it's about society ignoring it. When we reduce women to their appearance, sexual availability, or childbearing potential, we fail to recognize the lived experiences, insights, and wisdom they accumulate over time.

In professional spaces, this bias becomes even more glaring. Ageism often intersects with sexism, creating additional barriers for older women. Despite decades of experience, they are frequently overlooked for leadership positions or dismissed in favor of younger, often male, colleagues. The workplace, like other spheres, reinforces the notion that authority and competence age well in men but deteriorate in women.

Socially, older women are sidelined too. Family and community members may fail to seek their advice, assuming they are out of touch or irrelevant. This isolation robs younger generations of the wisdom and perspective older women carry, perpetuating a cycle where their contributions are undervalued or ignored entirely.

The truth is, the wisdom women gain as they age—relational, emotional, and intuitive—is a vital resource for families, communities, and workplaces. By dismissing it, patriarchy maintains its hold over who gets to be seen as an authority. Reclaiming the value of women's aging isn't just an act of personal empowerment; it's a cultural shift that requires us to see aging not as a loss but as a source of power.

Like the archetype of the wise woman or the old witch in the woods, aging women embody hard-earned knowledge and resilience, grounded in years of experience. Their wisdom is deeply relevant and transformative, even in a culture that tries to push it aside. When we reject the double standard and recognize aging as an accumulation of power, not its erosion, we reclaim a narrative that honors women's fullness at every stage of life.

The Cost of Devaluing the Aged

When we disregard the wisdom of our elders, particularly women, the consequences ripple throughout society in ways that are deeply damaging. The cost is far greater than the loss of individual voices—it is a collective loss that weakens our relationships, communities, spirituality, and even our connection to the environment and our spiritual heritage. When society chooses to value youth and productivity over the rich experiences and knowledge accumulated over a lifetime, we all suffer.

Ignoring the wisdom of older women creates a relational void. Elders who have done their healing work deeply understand resilience, relationships, and community-building that has been shaped over decades of lived experience. This is the kind of knowledge that cannot be learned through textbooks or quick fixes; it is cultivated through the ups and downs of life, through triumphs and losses, through the complexity of human relationships. Yet, when we dismiss or overlook older women's wisdom, we lose the ability to build stronger, more connected communities. Younger generations miss out on the opportunity to learn from those who have navigated the same paths before them, leaving them more vulnerable to making the same mistakes or feeling isolated in their struggles.

The cost isn't just emotional or relational—it's physical and environmental, too. Traditional practices, many of which have been passed down through generations of women, are often disregarded in favor of modern, extractive approaches that prioritize short-term gains over long-term sustainability. Women have historically been the keepers of knowledge about agriculture, food production, and natural medicines, understanding how to work with the earth in ways that ensure its replenishment for future generations. In many Indigenous and matriarchal societies, this wisdom is not just respected, it is essential to survival. When we disregard these practices, we lose not only the techniques themselves but also the values of sustainability and stewardship they carry. The environmental degradation we see today is, in part, a consequence of dismissing the wisdom of women who knew how to live in balance with the earth.

On a spiritual level, the loss is even more profound. In many Indigenous and matriarchal societies, women are the keepers of spiritual traditions, the ones who maintain the rituals, stories, and practices that connect the community to its roots and its sense of belonging. These traditions are not just relics of the past—they are living practices that provide meaning, guidance, and a sense of purpose. When we lose these spiritual practices, we become disconnected from our heritage, adrift in a world that prioritizes the material over the spiritual, the individual over the collective. We lose our sense of belonging to something greater than ourselves, and this spiritual disconnection can manifest as a sense of aimlessness or emptiness.

The individual costs of being disconnected from elder wisdom are just as severe. For younger women and nonbinary individuals, the absence of guidance from older generations can lead to feelings of emotional isolation, confusion, and burnout. Major life transitions—like puberty, motherhood, career changes, or even navigating the complexities of intimate relationships—become more difficult without the steady presence of someone who has been there before. When younger generations don't have access to the wisdom of their elders, they are left to figure things out on their own, which often leads to unnecessary struggles and hardships.

Moreover, when women are taught that their worth is tied to productivity, external achievements, or their physical appearance, aging seems like a loss of identity rather than a new season of wisdom. This leads to frustration, self-doubt, and a lack of confidence in their ability to navigate life's challenges. It also pits us against other wisdom by creating an underlying fear of being "replaced" by younger women in the roles we care about most. The result is a society filled with women who feel disconnected from their own wisdom, unsure of their place in the world, undervalued in both personal and professional spaces, and struggling to trust other women.

The patriarchal dismissal of women's wisdom, especially as they age, leaves a void in our society. The very qualities that could guide us through personal crises, environmental challenges, and spiritual disconnection are the ones we push to the margins. As a result, we find ourselves in a world that is not only less compassionate and connected but one that is unsustainable in the long run. Reclaiming the wisdom of aging women is not just a feminist or progressive act—it is a necessary step toward building a more balanced, sustainable, and spiritually rich society. When we begin to honor and reintegrate the wisdom of our elders, we create a future that is more inclusive, more sustainable, and more deeply connected to the values that truly matter.

The Contrast: Matriarchal and Indigenous Societies

While patriarchal societies tend to dismiss the wisdom of elders, especially women, many Indigenous and matriarchal cultures deeply revere their elders and recognize the immense value in the knowledge, experience, and insight they carry. In these societies, the aging process is often seen as a deepening of wisdom, not a diminishing of value. Older women hold an esteemed role as leaders, decision-makers, healers, and guides, and their wisdom is viewed as essential for the health and well-being of the community.

As mentioned above, in many matriarchal societies, older women are the primary keepers of cultural, spiritual, and practical knowledge. They are consulted on matters that affect the community, and their wisdom shapes decisions in areas like agriculture, medicine, education, and governance. Rather than being sidelined, they are revered as key contributors to the collective well-being and continuity of their people. Elders pass down stories, teachings, and practices that are vital to the community's identity and survival. Their guidance is sought in times of crisis, as their life experience offers perspectives younger generations may not have. The relational, emotional, and spiritual wisdom they carry helps communities stay connected to their roots and navigate challenges with resilience.

In many Indigenous communities, figures like *curanderas*—traditional healers in native Mexican cultures—embody this role of the wise elder and healer. Clarissa Pinkola Estés, herself a Curandera and a Jungian analyst, is best known for her groundbreaking book *Women Who Run with the Wolves*. She is also the author of numerous other books, lectures, and interviews that highlight the important role older women have always held—even when embracing that role was dangerous, risking marginalization or persecution like our old friend, the old witch in the woods.

The Old Woman (or Crone) archetype's roots in mythology and folklore reveal a rich legacy that, like the Curandera's, emphasizes the power of lived experience. In many traditions, both Crone and Curandera embody the culmination of a lifetime of challenges, growth, and insights. Far from being a figure of frailty or irrelevance, she is a keeper of deep truths and a guide through life's transitions. However, patriarchal societies have often misunderstood or vilified her, seeing her power as a threat. Far from being a figure of frailty or irrelevance, the Crone embodies the deep truths that come from embracing the cycles of life, death, and rebirth. She challenges societal norms that marginalize aging women and instead offers a model of resilience, authenticity, and unshakable wisdom.

Estés unapologetically fully embodies both Curandera and Crone, using her life and work to show the radical power and resilience of wise women.[1] She captures the essence of this wisdom and independence in her description of the Crone archetype: "She is the most dangerous, the most radical, the most revolutionary woman in existence. Whether in fairy tales or in reality, the old one goes where she wants to and she acts as she wishes; she lives as she chooses. And this is all as it should be. And no one can stop her."[2] The Crone's fierce independence aligns with the metaphor of the Old Witch in the Woods—a figure who lives beyond societal constraints, embodying an untamed wisdom that many fear but that others seek out in times of need.

Like the Old Witch in the Woods, these aging women exist on the edges of patriarchal society, in spaces where they can reclaim their power and influence. They serve as a bridge between modern and ancient worlds, guiding people to trust their instincts, reclaim their spiritual heritage, and reconnect with the wild, untamed aspects of their souls. This tradition of deep wisdom, passed down through women and rooted in ancestral knowledge, is a key aspect of how Indigenous and matriarchal societies uphold the value of older women.

These women, much like the Old Witch, show us that aging is not a process of fading into irrelevance but one of stepping into radical wisdom and unapologetic authenticity. Their stories and practices challenge societal norms, offering younger generations the courage to see aging not as a loss but as an initiation into a deeper, freer way of being. When we embrace our inner old witch in the woods, we reject the notion of diminishing worth with age and instead celebrate the richness of hard-earned wisdom that comes from a lifetime of experience.

Valuing the wisdom of women of mature age fosters a sense of intergenerational connection and continuity. These bonds create a sense of belonging, shared responsibility, and mutual respect among all members of the community. Younger generations gain access to a wealth of knowledge about resilience, survival, and relational living, fostering an environment of learning and growth where each generation contributes to the next.

In societies where women are respected as elders, they often serve as spiritual anchors. Their emotional and spiritual guidance keeps the community aligned with its traditions and values. They provide emotional support, serve as mediators during conflicts, and offer spiritual insight that helps individuals navigate personal challenges. By valuing older women, younger people are more secure in seeking advice, encouraging open communication, trust, and emotional well-being. Communities with this kind of support system are more resilient to external stressors—whether social, environmental, or economic—because they can draw upon the wisdom and insight of those who have already navigated similar challenges.

Aging women, having experienced a range of life's difficulties and triumphs, also serve as living examples of resilience and adaptability. When they are respected, their life stories become powerful tools for teaching younger generations about perseverance, problem-solving, and emotional strength. They model how to endure hardships with grace, how to celebrate life's joys fully, and how to adapt to the inevitable changes that come with time. This creates a community culture that values resilience and adaptability, empowering individuals to face challenges with the knowledge that they can rely on the collective wisdom of their elders.

In addition to emotional and spiritual guidance, elder women often hold the knowledge of sustainable living practices, particularly in Indigenous communities. They are the keepers of traditional knowledge about medicine, agriculture, and environmental stewardship. This wisdom, passed down through generations, ensures that cultural practices and ecological knowledge are preserved. By teaching younger generations how to live in harmony with nature, they foster sustainable practices that benefit both people and the planet. This creates a deep connection between the well-being of the community and the well-being of the natural world, reinforcing the idea that all life is interconnected.

When older women's wisdom is valued, individuals (particularly women) develop a strong sense of identity and purpose. They are raised in an environment where wisdom is shared freely, and personal growth is encouraged. Younger women benefit from seeing their elders as role models—living proof that their value goes beyond youth and that their contributions deepen with age. This helps individuals resist societal pressures to conform to superficial standards of beauty or success, allowing them to value their own experiences, knowledge, and potential for growth.

Author and Jungian analyst Sharon Blackie teaches, "the elder, fully embedded in and belonging to her place, is fierce in her protection of it. Love and respect your place, she will tell you, for there is a strong argument that you begin to love the whole—not just a pretty idea of Earth, but the complex thorny reality of it—by learning to fully love your own part."[3]

Like the old witch in the woods, our aging is visible to others and we get to choose how we respond to cultural pressures. Do we embrace our budding elder by loving every wrinkle, scar, and stretch mark? Do we lean into our wisdom and take up space in society? Do we choose to do the devastatingly hard work of mothering ourselves into and through a stage in life where Christian patriarchy tells us our value is diminishing?

By seeing aging as a natural and honorable process, individuals are more likely to embrace their own growth without fear. They can look forward to the future as a time of continued learning and contribution, rather than a period of decline. This shift in perspective enriches both individual lives and community well-being, creating a culture where wisdom, experience, and the gifts of aging are celebrated at every stage of life.

In contrast to patriarchal frameworks that prioritize youth and productivity, matriarchal and Indigenous societies offer a model of reverence for aging women, emphasizing their central role in community cohesion and well-being. When their wisdom is cherished and their contributions are recognized, everyone benefits.

The Individual Power of Embracing Aging

Aging is a journey that many of us feel hesitant to embrace, especially in a world that prizes youth over experience. Yet, with each year lived, we gather wisdom, resilience, and a deeper understanding of ourselves and the world. We unleash tremendous potential when we recognize this growth as an invitation to step into the power that comes with aging and to realize that, far from being a decline, it is a time when we can access profound insight, compassion, and strength.

Rejecting the cultural dismissal of aging and embracing the wisdom that comes with it profoundly impacts women at every stage of life. By learning from those who have walked before us, we reclaim our own authority, trust our experiences, and live more fully. Women, particularly, carry innate and acquired wisdom, and acknowledging this power can liberate us from the pressure to fit into narrow, age-based molds.

For younger women, this might mean cultivating the confidence to trust their intuition and recognize that their worth isn't tied to age or appearance. Middle-aged women can release the societal expectations to stay forever young and instead embrace the growth that comes from their lived experiences. For older women, this is a time to step fully into the role of wisdom keepers, mentors, and guides, sharing their insight with the world and refusing to be relegated to the background.

This journey begins by honoring the wisdom we've gained and seeing the beauty in every phase of life. It is about understanding that the fullness of our lived experience—whether in the boardroom, the classroom, or the home—is something no one can take from us. Embracing this means rejecting the narratives that tell us our value diminishes with age. It means celebrating the internal growth, emotional resilience, and deeper understanding that only time can bring.

Reclaiming and Celebrating Elders' Wisdom

Our elders hold the stories of our past and the seeds of our future. Even as they step into their later years, their wisdom doesn't fade—it deepens. But too often, we view aging as a process of decline, of being forgotten or set aside. Reframing this narrative allows us to see that elders, far from being pushed aside, are crucial sources of knowledge, connection, and healing.

Embracing elder wisdom doesn't only benefit the individual. It strengthens our communities. When we value our elders, we create a generational exchange that preserves culture, healing practices, and relational ways of living. Through storytelling, advice, and simply bearing witness, elders transmit lessons that enrich all who listen. This knowledge—gathered through decades of experience—is something no book or modern teaching can fully replicate. It's felt, lived, and understood in a way that transcends academic credentials.

Not everyone has access to living elders in their family, but that doesn't mean you can't still learn from the wisdom they carry. Even if your elders have passed or you've never had a close connection with them, there are still ways to tap into the deep well of knowledge they left behind.

Ways to Connect with Elders and Their Wisdom

- Study the lives of wise women in history: Many women who came before us broke barriers, challenged societal norms, and passed down legacies of strength and resilience. Explore their stories through books, podcasts, or documentaries to understand how they navigated aging and life's challenges.

- Build meaningful relationships with elders in your community: Whether they are family members, neighbors, or leaders, spend time listening to their stories. Ask about their life experiences, the lessons they've learned, and how they view the world today.
- Create a personal ritual to honor elders who have passed: Even without a genetic connection or memory of your elders, you can establish a spiritual practice of acknowledging their wisdom. Set aside time each week to reflect on what they might teach you, speak their names, or light a candle in their honor.
- Reflect on the teachings they imparted: Even if you don't have direct access to living elders, their wisdom lives on through memories, family traditions, or cultural heritage.
- Seek out wisdom through books or media: If you don't have elders in your life, look for stories of older women, particularly those who lived in matriarchal societies. Their experiences can offer invaluable lessons and inspire you to embrace aging with grace and dignity.

Reclaiming Aging as a Sacred Source of Wisdom and Healing

The personal impact of reclaiming aging and elder wisdom is transformative. Women who embrace their own aging process—rather than fighting it—experience a deep sense of freedom and empowerment. The process of aging becomes less about what's being lost and more about what's being gained: insight, understanding, and the ability to live life fully on one's own terms.

When we stop viewing aging as a loss of beauty or value, we start to appreciate the richness that comes with time. Instead of fearing the years ahead, we can look forward to a deeper sense of knowing—both of ourselves and the world. This shift in perspective doesn't just benefit the individual, but it also reshapes how society views women as they age. Rather than disappearing into the background, older women can take their rightful place as respected leaders, teachers, and guides.

Aging is a sacred journey into deeper wisdom, self-knowledge, and healing. When we reject the cultural narratives that devalue aging and instead honor the lived experiences of ourselves and our elders, we step into our power as wise women, ready to lead, mentor, and guide the next generation. By embracing the natural process of aging, we create a more compassionate, just, and balanced world where wisdom is valued at every stage of life.

Leaning In: Honoring the Through Line

I've created two activities for this chapter because it's important for you to explore your own aging and the legacy of your elders (living and passed, as well as chosen and birth families). If you've grown up in evangelical or fundamentalist Christianity, the idea of connecting with ancestors may feel foreign, strange, or even idolatrous. Many people in these faith communities are taught that our energy should only be directed toward God, and connecting with those who have passed on is seen as spiritually suspect.

However, what most modern Christianity misses is the deep and sacred connection we can still have with our ancestors, even after they have died. Across cultures and spiritual traditions, there is a long history of honoring those who came before us, recognizing the wisdom and experiences they carried, and acknowledging the profound impact they still have on our lives.

When we open ourselves to connecting with our ancestors, whether they are blood relatives or chosen family, we can begin to heal the wounds that have been passed down through generations. This practice allows us to reclaim wisdom that has been lost or suppressed and to deepen our understanding of who we are and where we come from. It also helps us embrace the fullness of our life stories, recognizing that we are part of a much larger narrative that includes those who came before us.

Healing intergenerational patterns and trauma doesn't just free us from the pain and limitations we've inherited—it also creates a healthier, more liberated path for future generations. When we confront and heal the wounds passed down through our families or communities, we break cycles of dysfunction, shame, and silence that might otherwise continue to affect us and those who come after us.

By healing these patterns, we're able to live more fully in the present, without the weight of unresolved trauma clouding our perceptions or decisions. We also benefit future generations by offering them a foundation rooted in wholeness, resilience, and emotional freedom. By healing ourselves, we transform the legacy we pass on, ensuring that our descendants—whether biological or chosen family—inherit wisdom, strength, and a clearer path to thriving, rather than the unresolved wounds of the past. This process not only reclaims the wisdom that's been lost but also opens the door to generational flourishing.

Activity 1: Reconnecting with Your Ancestors

This activity is designed to help you connect with your ancestors—whether they are blood relatives, chosen family, or spiritual ancestors—and begin the process of healing and reclaiming their wisdom.

1. Create a sacred space: Find a quiet, comfortable place where you can sit undisturbed for at least 10–15 minutes. Bring something meaningful that

connects you to your ancestors, such as a photo, a keepsake, a book they wrote, or a symbol that represents them.

2. Ground yourself: Close your eyes and take a few deep breaths. Visualize your body grounding into the earth, feeling rooted and connected to the wisdom that has been passed down through generations.
3. Call on your ancestors: Out loud, invite your ancestors—whether biological, adopted, or chosen—to be present with you. You might say, "I call on the wisdom of my ancestors, those known and unknown, to sit with me today."
4. Listen and reflect: Sit in silence for a few moments, opening your heart and mind to any feelings, memories, or messages that come to you. Trust whatever arises, even if it's subtle or doesn't make sense.
5. Journal: When you feel ready, write down what came up during your reflection. You might consider these prompts:
   - What came up inside me today?
   - What did my senses notice today (touch, taste, hearing, smell, sight)?
   - What did today's ancestor(s) want me to know, learn, or do?

By engaging in this practice regularly, you can strengthen your connection to your ancestors and allow their wisdom to guide your personal healing journey.

Activity 2: Meet Your Future Self

This activity is an opportunity to connect with your future self and reflect on the wisdom you want to carry forward as you age.

1. Find a quiet space: Sit comfortably in a place where you can reflect without distractions. Close your eyes, take a few deep breaths, and relax into the moment.
2. Visualize your future self: Picture yourself ten, twenty, or thirty years into the future. Visualize what you look like, where you are, and what your life feels like. Pay attention to the wisdom, peace, or strength that your future self embodies.
3. Reflect on wisdom: As you visualize, ask your future self:
   - What lessons have you learned about life and aging?
   - What wisdom do you hope to carry with you as you grow older?
   - How do you embrace the aging process with grace and confidence?
4. Journal your experience: After your visualization, take some time to write about what you saw and felt. Use these prompts to guide your journaling:
   - What did my future self teach me about aging and wisdom?
   - What values or practices will I cultivate to carry into the future?
   - How can I begin embracing aging with more acceptance and love today?

This activity will help you not only envision your future self but also provide insight into how you can live more fully in the present, guided by the wisdom you wish to carry forward.

Chapter 11

Reclaiming Your Roots

Early in this book, I told you I wasn't going to focus on other people's stories because we are working on your story—your inner narrative, truth, and healing. We've peeled back layers, confronted the harmful beliefs Christian patriarchy has ingrained in us, and started to reclaim pieces of ourselves buried beneath shame, fear, and control. Before we wrap up, however, there's one more essential conversation to have, and it does involve the stories of others—the stories of your ancestors. What's important here is not to get caught up in comparison or get distracted from our work. Instead, we need to hone in on how Christian patriarchy has shaped your connection to birth and chosen family.

As you read this chapter, your definition of family lineage may be challenged. Most of us are taught that ancestry is fixed and does not change. Lineage typically refers to your blood ancestors—the parents, grandparents, and great-grandparents who came before you. But both blood relatives and your chosen family shape your past, present, and future. As with all the other topics we've explored, I invite you to loosen your grip and get curious about how life might change if we view ourselves as the center of our lineage rather than the endpoint.

We are going to use a more expansive definition of lineage that acknowledges you are in the middle of your ancestral timeline. In this moment, you are both descendant and ancestor.

Lineage is our connection to those who came before us, those who are present in this life, and those who will follow.

Even if you are an only child with no children, you are not the end of your lineage. You are on a throughline that carries the stories of others and your stories will be carried by those who come after you.

This chapter isn't about lineage in the colonialist, patriarchal sense—a fixation on bloodlines, inheritance, and the hierarchical preservation of titles, wealth, or status. Instead, we're reclaiming lineage as a deeper, more soulful connection to our ancestors, our stories, and the legacies we're shaping every day. It's about honoring where we've come from and intentionally creating a path forward that reflects the values, wisdom, and change we want to seed for future generations. Lineage, in this context, is less about what we own and more about the stories we hold in our bodies and the legacy of healing or trauma we leave behind. Our ancestral healing journey is about finding deep connection to both ancestors and descendants and honoring the legacy we want to create.

Family Under Patriarchy

Christian patriarchy narrows the concept of family to a rigid structure built on control and submission, presenting an ideal that appears to celebrate family but ultimately prioritizes its hierarchical system. Sermons on "family values," conferences on patriarchal parenting, and messages about obedience within traditional roles all frame family as sacred, but this reverence is conditional. Family is valued only when it upholds patriarchal power dynamics. Women are encouraged to pursue their "calling," but only if it aligns with the role of a submissive wife and long-suffering mother.

In this structure, family becomes less a sanctuary of connection and more a mechanism for enforcing conformity. Rather than honoring each person's uniqueness, Christian patriarchy defines family as a system where authority rests solely in the hands of men. Love and acceptance often feel transactional, contingent on adherence to prescribed roles. Fathers are the heads of households, mothers are relegated to "helpmeet" status, and children are expected to follow obediently. Deviations from this "natural order" are met with resistance, correction, or even ostracism, turning family into a controlled microcosm of the larger patriarchal society.

Under this framework, emotional needs are acknowledged only when they reinforce patriarchal values. Women are expected to suppress anger or dissatisfaction, while those who don't are dismissed as rebellious. Men, meanwhile, are discouraged from showing vulnerability, forced instead to embody a narrow version of "biblical masculinity" that prioritizes authority over emotional presence. Support and affection are often withheld as tools of correction, and love becomes less a gift freely given and more a reward for conforming to expectations.

This limited, transactional view of family strips it of its potential to nurture genuine connection and mutual growth. Instead, it creates a closed system that isolates family members from themselves and each other. "Honoring" family, as Christian patriarchy defines it, equates to unwavering submission to authority, often at the expense of personal truth, individuality, and well-being. In this dynamic, power and control replace the nurturing support that family could otherwise provide, severing its ability to be a space for healing and growth.

Even within patriarchal families, love is often deep and genuine, but it can be shaped by unspoken rules that uphold the existing hierarchy. Individualism and emotional connection may be encouraged—but only within boundaries that reinforce traditional roles. A child's curiosity might be celebrated, for example, so long as it doesn't question authority. A woman's strength may be valued when it supports her role as a wife or mother but dismissed when it challenges the family structure. These limitations create a subtle yet pervasive pressure to conform, often at the expense of authenticity and genuine self-expression.

This rigidity fragments the deeper, natural connections we share with one another, our ancestors, and our inner wisdom. Patriarchal systems benefit from this isolation, weakening the collective strength of these relationships. The archetype of the "old witch in the woods"—a wise, self-possessed woman cast out for her knowledge and power—symbolizes this disconnection. Just as the old witch represents resistance to control, our ability to connect authentically with our family and lineage empowers us to defy systems designed to isolate us from inherited strength and wisdom.

It's important to acknowledge that families in patriarchal systems often deeply love one another and strive for connection, but even in the most loving families, patriarchal norms can impose limitations that restrict the full expression of love and support. Emotional needs that don't align with these norms are often ignored or met with suspicion, and affection may be withheld to enforce compliance. This dynamic reduces family relationships to a kind of conditional love, where individuality and authenticity are sacrificed to maintain the prescribed order.

True family connection has the potential to be transformative—a source of healing, empowerment, and mutual growth. But this potential can only be realized when we move beyond the limitations imposed by patriarchal systems. Families thrive when they become spaces where individuality is honored, emotions are freely expressed, and love is unconditional. Reclaiming this vision of family challenges the control-based dynamics of Christian patriarchy, creating the possibility for deeper, more authentic connections that nurture everyone involved.

Conditional Love and the Hierarchy of Control

In Christian patriarchy, individuals who step outside prescribed roles often face severe consequences. Whether someone rejects traditional gender norms, comes out as 2SLGBTQIA+, questions the authority of church leaders, or challenges patriarchal values, such acts of defiance under this system threaten the family hierarchy. In response, families may withdraw love or cut off relationships, creating deep fractures that reinforce submission and discourage independence.

This programming is harmful, teaching us from a young age that love is conditional and that approval is something we must earn by conforming to certain standards. We learn to suppress our true selves to maintain relationships, continually adjusting to meet the family's expectations rather than expressing who we are. In prioritizing authority over personal authenticity, Christian patriarchy deepens our disconnection from ourselves and others, entrenching us in a cycle of isolation, control, and assimilation.

The message is clear: To gain acceptance, we must submit, seeking approval from the very figures who enforce this limiting system. This control over love and connection isn't isolated within families; it permeates the larger Christian patriarchal structure, creating a self-sustaining system where our identities are rooted not in self-worth but in compliance with hierarchical expectations.

The Erosion of Authentic Connection

What gets lost in all of this is authentic connection. When family becomes a means of enforcing hierarchy and submission, it strips away the possibility for real, vulnerable, mutual relationships. Christian patriarchy teaches that family is essential, but only in the ways that serve its control. It doesn't teach us to deeply connect with our ancestors, honor their wisdom, or engage in the healing work that lineage requires.

This narrow view of family creates a self-sustaining cycle where we pass down the same harmful beliefs and behaviors rather than creating a legacy of healing and transformation.

The teachings don't promote a deep engagement with our ancestors' lives, struggles, or triumphs; instead, they offer a surface-level notion of lineage that reinforces a hierarchical, obedience-based structure. It's a disconnection that limits us from exploring the richness of our ancestors' stories or creating a legacy of healing and transformation.

This disconnection is intentional. Christian patriarchy knows that when we are disconnected from our lineage, we are easier to control. When we're isolated from our true heritage—separated from the web of ancestors, siblings, and descendants—we become more susceptible to the restrictive narratives we've been fed. We are more likely to believe that our worth is determined by how well we adhere to patriarchal norms rather than by the strength, resilience, and wisdom that we've inherited from those who came before us.

We forget our ancestors' resilience, strength, and wisdom lies within us and begin to believe our worth depends solely on how well we fit into the patriarchal mold.

Reclaiming Lineage Beyond Patriarchy

Reclaiming our connection to our lineage means rejecting the narrow, hierarchical definitions of family that Christian patriarchy imposes. It means understanding that our connection to our ancestors and descendants is not about submission or obedience but about mutual healing, growth, support, and transformation. It means recognizing that we are part of a lineage that extends far beyond the confines of patriarchal control and that our healing has the power to flow through generations—both backward and forward in time.

When we embrace this broader, more expansive understanding of family, we begin to see that lineage is not just about bloodlines or biological connections. It's about the stories, traditions, and wisdom that have been passed down to us. It's about our foremothers' resilience, our ancestors' survival, and the strength that flows through us today. And it's about the legacy we are creating for future generations—the legacy of healing, wholeness, and liberation.

In this way, family becomes more than just a mechanism for control—it becomes a source of power, connection, and healing. It becomes a way for us to root ourselves in the wisdom of the past while also creating a future where our descendants know how to unbind themselves from the wounds of patriarchy. By reclaiming our lineage, we reclaim our power. We become part of something larger than ourselves, part of a continuum of healing that stretches across time and space.

When we embrace our role in the middle of our lineage, we once again call forth the old witch in the woods—the wise woman who lives beyond the limitations of patriarchal family structures. She is untamed, deeply rooted, and unaffected by society's expectations of obedience or submission. In her wisdom, she transcends hierarchies and embodies a lineage of self-trust, intuition, and liberation. Through her, we find inspiration to reclaim our lineage as an expansive space of belonging, rooted in the freedom to honor our ancestors' truths as well as our own. Through her, we can begin to create a better future.

When we recognize that lineage is about connection rather than control, we can begin to heal the wounds that Christian patriarchy has inflicted on our families. We can reconnect with our ancestors in ways that honor their wisdom and resilience. We can create new, healthy, and authentic connections with our descendants. And in doing so, we can break free from the cycle of shame, fear, and disconnection that has held us captive for so long.

By embracing lineage as a sacred and healing force, we reject the limitations that Christian patriarchy places on family, and begin to forge new paths of connection, both to those who came before us and to those who will come after. We become the ancestors our descendants will one day look to for guidance, strength, and wisdom, knowing that we have done the healing work necessary to pass on a legacy of love, liberation, and wholeness.

The Expansive Nature of Lineage

So, what is it about lineage that's so threatening to Christian patriarchy? The answer is simple: An unrestricted connection to our lineage roots us to the past, the present, and the future. It reminds us that no one lives in isolation—our actions ripple outward, affecting far more than just ourselves. We exist in a complex, interconnected web of ancestors, siblings, and descendants. We are the culmination of hundreds, possibly thousands, of cultural traditions and personal experiences that shape who we are today.

This interconnectedness poses a direct challenge to Christian patriarchy because it decentralizes authority and control. Christian patriarchy often emphasizes a narrow view of lineage rooted in obedience to God and male leadership. By contrast, a broader understanding of lineage affirms multiple sources of wisdom, including our ancestors, the earth, and the collective experiences of humanity. While Christianity offers a hope that spans past, present, and future, its patriarchal interpretations frequently frame that hope within a hierarchical structure. Acknowledging the expansive nature of lineage disrupts this framework, allowing individuals—especially women—to access spiritual, cultural, and personal power outside the control of patriarchal gatekeepers.

Even if you've never met your birth parents or are entirely cut off from your genetic family tree, your lineage lives inside you. It shapes how you walk through the world. Our bodies carry the memories, joys, traumas, and resilience of those who came before us, whether we know it or not.

The healing work we've done throughout this book—the work you've been doing—has the power to shift things far beyond your own life. It can change the way your genes are expressed, release the trauma of loved ones who have passed, and alter the trajectory of those who come after you. It sounds a little witchy, doesn't it? A little mystical and magical?

As author Arthur C. Clarke famously said, "Magic is just science we don't understand yet."[1] The magic of how our body connects to our ancestors and descendants is starting to be understood by science in very tangible ways.

Epigenetics: The Science of Inherited Trauma

Let's talk about epigenetics. This relatively new field of science is revealing profound truths about how our genetic code isn't as static as we once believed. For years, we were taught that our DNA was fixed—that the genes we inherited were unchangeable, locked in place from birth. But epigenetics is flipping that narrative on its head. Our genes, it turns out, are not set in stone. They are influenced by the experiences, traumas, and even joys of those who came before us.

What's most fascinating about epigenetics is that it shows how the lives of our ancestors—what they ate, how they lived, the trauma they endured—affect the biological makeup of our bodies today. This is not just metaphorical; it's real, measurable science. Our genes carry the echoes of the past, and the choices and experiences of our ancestors have shaped us in ways we are only beginning to understand.

Take, for example, studies conducted on the descendants of Holocaust survivors. A study led by Dr. Rachel Yehuda at the Icahn School of Medicine at Mount Sinai examined thirty-two Jewish individuals who survived Nazi concentration camps, experienced torture, or hid during World War II, along with their children.[2] The research found epigenetic changes in both survivors and their offspring at the same site of the FKBP5 gene, which is involved in stress response regulation. Interestingly, while survivors exhibited increased methylation at this site, their children showed decreased methylation, indicating that the trauma-induced epigenetic modifications were inherited but manifested differently in the next generation.

Essentially, the children's genes "remember" the trauma of their grandparents, even though they never directly experienced it themselves. The same has been found in studies of descendants of enslaved people,[3] as well as in Indigenous communities that have endured centuries of colonization, displacement, and genocide.[4]

The trauma your ancestors faced doesn't just disappear—it impacts the expression of their DNA, and those genetic influences are passed down through the generations. This means that the anxiety, fear, or chronic health conditions you may struggle with today could, in part, be the result of ancestral trauma that has been inherited.

Epigenetics is giving us the language to understand why so many of us carry the weight of histories we didn't personally live through but still feel deeply. It's why certain patterns seem to repeat in families, why certain emotional responses feel so ingrained. The trauma isn't just emotional—it's biological, embedded in the very structure of our cells. And while that might sound daunting, here's where the magic really happens: Just as trauma can be inherited, healing can be passed down, too.

When we engage in healing work—whether it's through therapy, spiritual practice, or simply breaking generational cycles—we aren't just healing ourselves. We are healing the epigenetic markers that were passed down to us. And in doing so, we are also shifting the genetic legacy we will pass on to future generations. Your healing today has the power to change the genetic expression of your children and grandchildren. You are rewriting the story, not just for yourself but for your entire lineage.

This is why the work you've been doing—unraveling the harmful beliefs, releasing the shame, reclaiming your body and your truth—is so much bigger than you. Every step you take toward healing is a step toward breaking the cycles of trauma that have been passed down for generations. And in doing so, you are offering future generations the gift of a healthier, more empowered, and more liberated lineage.

Rabbi Tirzah Firestone's Work on Ancestral Healing

One of the greatest resources on ancestral healing comes from Rabbi Tirzah Firestone,[5] who has spent decades studying inherited trauma, particularly among Holocaust survivors and their descendants. In her groundbreaking book *Wounds into Wisdom*, she explores how the trauma of the Holocaust didn't end with the survivors—it was passed down, shaping the lives of the survivors' children and grandchildren in ways they couldn't fully understand. Firestone refers to this intergenerational trauma as the "unresolved life experiences" that "reverberate within us and shape us."[6] This trauma, she explains, affects us not only on an individual level but also on a collective one, weaving itself into the fabric of families and communities.

Rabbi Firestone's work is not just about identifying inherited trauma—it's about healing it. She teaches that we can transform our inherited wounds into sources of wisdom and strength. This transformation doesn't happen by ignoring the trauma or pretending it didn't affect us. It happens by facing it head-on, acknowledging the pain and suffering of our ancestors, and recognizing how those experiences have shaped our lives today.

One of the most powerful concepts in Rabbi Firestone's work is the idea that trauma isn't the only inheritable trait. Yes, we inherit the wounds of our ancestors, but we also inherit their resilience, their courage, and their capacity for healing. The strength it took for them to survive is passed down to us, just as surely as the trauma is. And when we engage in the process of healing—when we turn our wounds into wisdom—we aren't just healing ourselves. We are healing our entire lineage.

The children and grandchildren of Holocaust survivors, for example, often carry a deep, unspoken sense of anxiety or fear, a kind of inherited hypervigilance. But Rabbi Firestone also points out that this hypervigilance is a sign of something deeper: the will to survive. Our ancestors didn't just pass down their trauma—they passed down their will to live and their determination to keep going, even in the face of unimaginable suffering. That will, that determination, is what allows us to heal.

Healing intergenerational trauma is not just about healing the past—it's about transforming the future. Rabbi Firestone emphasizes that the work we do to heal our ancestral wounds doesn't just stop with us. It ripples out through the generations, altering the trajectory of our descendants. We have the power to transform the legacy we pass down, turning inherited trauma into inherited resilience.

Rabbi Firestone's work reminds us that healing is both an individual and a collective process. When we heal ourselves, we heal the wounds of our ancestors. In doing so, we create a new legacy for those who come after us—one rooted in strength, wisdom, and love.

Ancestral Healing: A Sacred and Holy Process

Before we go any further, let's clarify something: Engaging in ancestral healing does not mean replacing God with your grandmother. It's not about ancestor worship in the way Christian patriarchy fears. It's about recognizing that the work we do to heal ourselves is part of a sacred and holy process that honors the lives of those who came before us and prepares the way for those who will come after us.

Ancestral healing is about reclaiming the wisdom, resilience, and strength of those who survived before us. We acknowledge that their struggles and triumphs shaped the path we walk today and that we have the power to shift that path for the future.

Challenging Christian Patriarchy's Heaven and Hell

Reclaiming our place in an expansive lineage directly contradicts Christian patriarchy's goal of keeping us focused on a narrow path of obedience between heaven and hell. By encouraging us to see heaven and hell as literal places—final destinations of reward or punishment—Christian patriarchy establishes a system where absolute compliance to God's will (as dictated by patriarchal interpretation) is the only acceptable aim. This doctrine redirects our attention away from personal and ancestral connection, isolating us from our roots and the expansive, enduring nature of our lineage.

The concept of hell has evolved over time, shaped by influences from both Jewish and Greek afterlife traditions. In its earliest form, Jewish theology described Sheol, a shadowy, silent pit where all the dead—righteous and wicked alike—lingered in a minimal state of existence outside the presence of God. By the sixth century BCE, Sheol transformed into a temporary holding place where the departed awaited resurrection, with the righteous joining God and the wicked suffering fiery torment in Gehenna, a valley outside of Jerusalem that was used as a dumping ground and was usually described as a place of fire and smoke.

Ancient Greek beliefs similarly envisioned Hades, an underworld where spirits languished in a twilight existence. Those guilty of great evildoing faced punishment in Tartarus, a deeper realm of gloom. After Alexander the Great's conquest of Judea in the fourth century BCE, these Greek ideas became part of Jewish and later Christian awareness. Jesus, as recorded in the Gospels, refers to the Jewish concept of Gehenna as a place of eternal fire and to Hades in the context of the struggle against evil. These early influences show that hell was initially more symbolic—a representation of separation from the Divine and the consequences of sin.

Contrasting Patriarchy with a Lineage-Centered Worldview

By enforcing a strict interpretation, Christian patriarchy uses heaven and hell to create a linear, obedience-driven life model where we focus solely on "earning" our place in the afterlife rather than finding meaning in our interconnected lineage on earth. This doctrine isolates individuals from personal and ancestral connection, redirecting focus to compliance with a narrow set of rules rather than honoring shared humanity and collective wisdom.

Such a reductive view stands in stark contrast to the powerful sense of belonging and continuity that a broader understanding of lineage provides. We see ourselves as both ancestors to future generations and descendants of those who came before, embodying qualities and strengths inherited through the ages.

Recognizing ourselves as part of an enduring spiritual lineage enriches our lives, rooting us in a legacy of divine love and restoration.

Embracing this expansive view of lineage heals our connection to the past, restores our sense of wholeness, and transforms the legacy we leave behind. When we see ourselves as part of a long line of survivors, creators, healers, and warriors, we recognize that we carry their strength as much as their struggles. With this awareness, we become part of a larger healing process that reshapes the future for generations.

By valuing growth, healing, and integrity over fear-driven obedience, we cultivate lives that honor our interconnected lineage, offering meaning and strength rooted in shared humanity. This worldview opens us to a life of purpose that transcends fear and control, grounding us in a legacy of love and continuity that patriarchal systems cannot co-opt. Reclaiming lineage as something timeless—woven with both past and future—shifts our focus from solitary obedience to a life of connection.

Moving Forward with Respect and Responsibility

As you continue your journey of healing, I invite you to explore your lineage with humility and respect. Reconnect with your ancestors' stories, seek out traditional wisdom rooted in your heritage, and approach this process with reverence. Avoid the temptation to appropriate or commodify practices that don't belong to you and instead focus on honoring the sacredness of your own lineage. This is especially important for those of us who come from white, European-descended backgrounds. We need to be careful not to fall into the trap of saying, "Well, my grandma was one-fourth Cherokee" as a way of laying claim to traditions that aren't ours.

The goal here is not to exploit or commodify the practices of Indigenous cultures or those deemed "exotic" by the West. Too often, spiritual practices have been stripped from their sacred roots and promoted by people who have no connection to them—people who have not been trained by Indigenous communities and don't carry the responsibility of those practices, but who use them as a way to make money or gain power. This is not what we are doing here.

Instead, we must take a humble position, acknowledging the legacy of white supremacy, colonization, stolen resources, and the genocide of marginalized people around the world by descendants of white Europeans. We must own the harm that has been done and seek to learn from sources with deep connections to the traditions we seek to honor. This means seeking out the healers, *curanderas*, and elders within our own ancestral communities (both living and dead) rather than appropriating practices that don't belong to us. You can find a list of suggested places to begin on my website.[7] Members of other cultures may invite us into some experiences, but the key here is that those invitations are not assumed or demanded. Use the sexual consent rule as your guideline here: If it's not an enthusiastic yes, it's a no. Stand back and appreciate the culture as an outsider.

Honoring our lineage is about reconnecting with the stories, rituals, and wisdom that resonate deeply because they are part of who we are, not because they are trendy or exotic. When we approach this process with humility and respect, we honor the sacredness of the healing work we are doing.

You are part of something bigger than yourself. The healing work you are doing now will ripple through generations. Your ancestors are with you, as is the seed of your descendants that will carry forward the legacy of healing you are creating.

As we wrap up this chapter, take a moment to reflect on the strength, wisdom, and love that flow through your lineage. You are not alone in this journey. You are part of a sacred, interconnected web that stretches through time and space.

By reconnecting to your roots, you are reclaiming the wholeness that Christian patriarchy tried to sever. And in doing so, you are not just healing yourself—you are healing your ancestors, your descendants, and the entire lineage that flows through you.

Leaning In: The Family Reunion

This activity invites you to envision a family reunion where everyone—your ancestors and descendants, whether by birth, chosen, or symbolic—comes together. At this gathering, you're not just a participant but a central part of the lineage, a through-point where stories, wisdom, and connection flow freely.

Step 1: Set the Scene

Close your eyes and imagine a table in a welcoming space. This could be a familiar family home, a favorite spot in nature, or a place that feels symbolic of belonging and comfort. Picture the table being long enough for everyone who wants to join—ancestors on one side and descendants on the other, with you seated right in the middle.

The table fills with those who've shaped your past and those who will carry your legacy forward. Some faces may be familiar, while others might represent energies or traits you've inherited or will pass on. Let the table feel expansive and inclusive, open to anyone who brings wisdom, connection, or love.

Step 2: Start the Conversation

As the reunion begins, imagine the group settling into a relaxed rhythm of sharing stories. At first, let the conversation flow naturally, then guide it with these prompts:

- To your ancestors:
    - What stories do you want me to remember?
    - What values or lessons have shaped our lineage?
    - Is there anything in our shared history that needs healing or acknowledgment?
- To your descendants:
    - What kind of legacy do you hope I leave for you?
    - What strengths or wisdom do you see in me that you hope to carry forward?
    - How can I nurture the path for you, even in small ways?

Feel free to take notes or simply absorb the energy of the exchange. Let the stories, emotions, and insights flow freely, knowing this is a space where everyone belongs.

Step 3: Reflect on What You've Heard

After the imagined reunion, take time to reflect. Think about the connections and stories shared at the table and consider:

- What themes or lessons stood out to you?
- What strengths or gifts do you see flowing through your lineage?
- What wounds or challenges surfaced, and how can you begin to heal them?

Write down any key insights or takeaways. Let this reflection remind you of the richness and complexity of your lineage—both the joys and the struggles.

Step 4: Honor the Reunion

To honor this gathering and your place in the lineage, create a tangible reminder of the reunion. This could be:

- A memento from the table: Imagine leaving the table with a symbolic gift—a story, a piece of wisdom, or an imagined object that represents your connection to your lineage.
- A shared tradition: Start or continue a tradition that reflects the values or stories shared during the reunion. It might be as simple as lighting a candle, sharing a meal, or telling a favorite family story.
- A personal commitment: Write down one or two ways you'll honor the connections in your lineage—perhaps by living a value expressed at the reunion or sharing stories with others.

Step 5: Carry the Reunion Forward

Remember, the energy of this imagined reunion is always available to you. When life feels overwhelming or disconnected, picture the table again. Revisit the wisdom, strength, and love that were shared there.

Ask yourself:

- How can I honor the wisdom I've inherited in my daily life?
- What legacy do I want to shape for those who come after me?
- How can I keep the stories and values of my lineage alive?

This reunion reminds you that you're not alone. You're part of a lineage that stretches across time, shaped by those who came before and those who will come after. By holding space for these connections, you're creating a legacy of healing, love, and authenticity—a gift to your ancestors, your descendants, and yourself.

Chapter 12

Choosing Your Path Forward

As we come to the close of this book, I want to be clear that this journey is not just a one-time awakening but the beginning of a deeper transformation. Through these pages, you've explored how the traits that society often undervalues in women—intuition, emotions, wisdom, and the beauty of aging—are not weaknesses but profound sources of connection, insight, and resilience. Christian patriarchy and other oppressive systems have tried to convince us that our natural strengths are somehow flawed or unworthy. These beliefs have encouraged us to make ourselves smaller, to dim our innate brilliance. But that narrative is false.

The truth is, women have always been carriers of wisdom, caretakers of collective well-being, and voices of vision and healing. We don't need to fit into rigid expectations to make a meaningful impact; we simply need to reclaim what has always been within us—our inner knowing, emotional depth, and lived experiences. This chapter is an invitation to explore a path that honors all of who we are. It's about recognizing why systems of control work so hard to stifle these gifts and how choosing to nurture our inherent strengths will lead us toward lives of freedom, connection, and fulfillment.

Reclaiming and Honoring Our Natural Strengths

The qualities that patriarchal society has diminished or deemed undesirable—our intuition, emotional depth, caregiving instincts, and even the natural process of aging—are not undervalued because they are weak but because they hold incredible power. These traits are vital sources of strength and grounding, yet oppressive systems thrive by convincing us otherwise. By marginalizing women's qualities, patriarchy preserves its control, subtly suggesting that women's wisdom and insight are somehow secondary.

Consider what we've unpacked together: how emotions are mislabeled as "too much," how aging is framed as a loss rather than the deepening of understanding, and how knowledge has been withheld to maintain control. Those times you were dismissed, belittled, or shamed, weren't just incidental but woven into a broader pattern designed to hold back women's full expression. If society can dismiss women's emotions as "irrational," it becomes easier to disregard women's voices. When women's wisdom is downplayed as less rational than intellectual achievement, it creates an implicit hierarchy that favors the masculine over the feminine, sidelining women's contributions to community and culture.

This suppression is more than personal; it's institutional. Religious, social, and political structures have worked to reinforce a single story: that men are designed to guide while women are meant to follow. In Christian patriarchy, this narrative is often supported by selective interpretations of Scripture, promoting women's subjugation as not only acceptable but virtuous.

Yet, at our core, we know that these qualities—our emotions, intuition, caregiving, and wisdom—are rich sources of strength and wholeness. When we embrace our emotional intelligence, we show up with empathy and insight, creating spaces that are safe, inclusive, and nurturing. When we honor the wisdom that comes with age and experience, we bring grounded and insightful perspectives. When we trust our intuition, we are guided by logic and a profound alignment with our deepest truths. This reclamation is healing for us individually and transformative for our families, communities, and the generations that will follow.

The Choice to Continue the Work

It's easy to feel empowered in the middle of a journey like this as we read, reflect, and learn about the systems of oppression that have shaped our lives. Perhaps you're feeling that now, as you near the end of this book. But what happens after the book is closed—after the last page is read, and the world creeps back in with its noise, demands, and expectations? This is where the real work begins.

The path of healing and liberation is not linear and certainly not easy. It's a process of unlearning everything you've been taught about your worth and place in the world—and relearning who you truly are. It's about challenging the external and internal voices that tell you to play small, be quiet, and defer to others. It's about choosing, again and again, to keep going—even when it feels overwhelming.

There will be moments when you doubt yourself. There will be times when the pressure to conform feels suffocating, and you'll wonder if it would be easier to go back to the way things were. But every time you choose to trust yourself, every time you choose to reject the lies that patriarchy has fed you, you step closer to freedom.

This work is not just for you. It's for those who came before you and those who will come after. When you choose to do this work, you are part of a larger movement to dismantle systems of oppression to create a world where women, nonbinary people, and marginalized voices are heard, valued, and celebrated. And this is work worth doing. It's work worth continuing, even when it feels hard.

Spiritual practices are essential to sustaining yourself in this work. In a world that constantly pulls at our attention, asks us to conform, and tells us we are not enough, we need spaces where we can reconnect with our inner wisdom and nourish our souls. But for many of us, our spiritual practices have been shaped by the very systems we are trying to dismantle.

It's important to reflect on the spiritual practices you've inherited and ask yourself: Do these practices bring me life? Do they help me reconnect with my inherent worth? Or do they reinforce the patriarchal control I'm trying to break free from? It's okay to let go of the practices that no longer serve you. It's okay to create new spiritual rhythms that align with your journey toward healing and liberation.

Consider what spiritual practices feel nourishing to you. Maybe it's journaling, where you can process your emotions and reflect on your growth. Perhaps it's meditation, where you ground yourself in the present moment and listen to your inner voice. Or maybe it's spending time in nature, where you can reconnect with the cycles of life and remember that aging and change are natural and beautiful processes.

Whatever practices you choose, the key is to make space for rest, joy, and reflection. These are not indulgences—they are essential to your well-being. Rest is an act of resistance in a world that values productivity over humanity. Joy is a declaration that you are worthy of pleasure and delight, no matter what the world tells you. Reflection is a way to stay connected to your path, remember why you started, and continue moving forward with intention.

One way to stay grounded in this process is to remind yourself why you started. Reflect on what you've learned and how far you've come. Journal about the moments of clarity you've experienced, the lies you've uncovered, and the truths you are beginning to embrace. These reflections can serve as a compass when the path feels unclear, guiding you back to your center and reminding you that you are on a journey of liberation.

Here's a quick recap of each topic we tackled to help you quickly reference what you've learned as you create or lean into spiritual practices that nourish you. Each section offers a reminder of what Christian patriarchy says, what you now know to be true, and what's possible if you lean into the truth.

Embodiment: Reclaiming the Sacredness of Your Body

Patriarchy says your body is an object to be controlled, criticized, and commodified, but you know your body is a sacred vessel that carries your intuition, strength, and power.

Embracing embodiment means tuning into the deep wisdom your body offers you every day, listening to its signals, and honoring its needs. It means reclaiming your physicality as a source of grounding and joy, not something to be reshaped or hidden to meet society's impossible standards. When you sit in the power of embodiment, you unlock the ability to live more fully in the present, trusting your body's innate wisdom and recognizing it as a site of divine connection.

Imagine the freedom of confidently moving through life, knowing that your body is not only enough but a source of tremendous strength and insight.

Mothering: The Power of Nurturing Beyond Traditional Roles

Patriarchy says mothering is about self-sacrifice, submission, and fulfilling duties, but you know mothering is an act of radical creation and nurturing that extends far beyond biological roles.

Mothering is not confined to raising children—it is the ability to nurture life, ideas, communities, and yourself. It is the power to cultivate growth and provide care where it is most needed. By redefining mothering, you step into the sacred role of a creator, not one shackled by patriarchal expectations but one who nurtures from a place of abundance and intention.

Imagine how life will flourish when you mother from a place of self-love and empowerment, choosing how and where you invest your nurturing energy.

Self-Nourishing: The Sacred Act of Caring for Yourself

Patriarchy says that caring for yourself is selfish or indulgent, but now you know that self-nourishment is essential for your well-being and a revolutionary act of self-preservation.

True nourishment means more than simply resting or eating well—it is about honoring your needs on every level: emotional, spiritual, and physical. When you fiercely protect your ability to nourish yourself, you tap into a wellspring of resilience and balance.

Imagine the peace and strength you'll carry when you no longer feel guilty for putting yourself first and instead embrace self-nourishment as a sacred practice that allows you to pour from a full cup.

Pleasure: Reclaiming Joy as a Birthright

Patriarchy says pleasure is dangerous, indulgent, or something to be earned, but you know pleasure is your birthright and a sacred path to connecting with your true self, your creator, and your community.

Pleasure is not just physical—it is the joy of being alive, of experiencing beauty, connection, and wonder in all its forms. Embracing pleasure means rejecting the idea that you must earn joy or suppress your desires to be worthy. When you own your pleasure, you tap into an infinite source of vitality and creativity.

Imagine living in a world where your joy is not conditional but where you move through life as a beacon of unapologetic pleasure and delight in all the small and large wonders of life.

Emotions: Honoring the Full Spectrum of Your Feelings

Patriarchy says your emotions make you weak or irrational, but you know your emotions are powerful teachers and sacred guides to your inner world.

Emotions are not to be suppressed or feared; they are pathways to deeper understanding and connection with yourself and others. When you embrace the full range of your emotions—joy, sorrow, anger, and everything in between—you reclaim your wholeness. Imagine the strength that comes from honoring your emotional experiences as valid and necessary, learning to sit with each feeling and recognize the wisdom it brings. You'll be able to move through the world with greater emotional intelligence, depth, and authenticity, leading a life that honors your true feelings.

Autonomy: Standing in the Power of Self-Governance

Patriarchy says you must be controlled, guided, or led by others, but you know autonomy is your sacred right to live and lead your life in alignment with your core values, beliefs, and desires.

Autonomy means owning your decisions, trusting your intuition, and leading your life from a place of self-governance. It is the freedom to define your path, free from the expectations or control of others. When you embrace your autonomy, you unlock the power to live authentically, rejecting the narratives that have sought to keep you small. Imagine how your life will expand when you fully trust your capacity to lead yourself, to choose your direction, and to honor your own voice without external validation.

Wisdom: Recognizing Your Innate and Learned Knowledge

Patriarchy says your wisdom is inferior, particularly if it doesn't come from approved academic sources, but you know that your wisdom—both innate and learned—is vast, intuitive, and deeply valuable.

Wisdom isn't only found in books or degrees; it's in lived experiences, spiritual insight, and intuitive knowing. When you trust your wisdom, you recognize that your perspective is unique, rich, and necessary for the world. Imagine stepping fully into your power, knowing that your knowledge is enough—that your understanding of life and the world has a rightful place in shaping your decisions and guiding others. You can confidently bring your voice to the table, knowing it carries the weight of your sacred experiences.

Aging: Embracing the Sacred Journey of Aging

Patriarchy says aging means losing value, becoming irrelevant, or being cast aside, but you know that aging is a sacred journey into deeper wisdom, power, and grace.

Aging is not a decline—it's a process of gathering strength, insight, and experience that enriches your life and the lives of others. With every passing year, you accumulate more wisdom and understanding, becoming a deeper well of knowledge and spiritual richness. Imagine rejecting the fear of aging and instead embracing each year as a rite of passage into greater authority, wisdom, and influence. When you honor your aging process, you set a powerful example for younger generations, showing them that growing older is a beautiful and sacred journey.

You step fully into your divine, authentic self by reclaiming these sacred aspects of yourself—your embodiment, nurturing power, pleasure, autonomy, emotions, wisdom, and aging. You dismantle the oppressive narratives that have sought to limit you, and in their place, you create a life filled with joy, strength, and deep spiritual fulfillment.

You are not only capable of flourishing in this sacred power, but you also deserve it. Every step you take in honoring these traits leads you closer to a life of purpose, connection, and freedom.

Community Support and Collective Growth

Healing is not something that happens in isolation. No matter how deeply we work on ourselves, our personal liberation is intimately tied to the communities we belong to. The support we receive from those who truly see and honor us can be transformative, helping to break the cycles of oppression and empowering us to reclaim our fullness. Building equitable relationships is essential for individual healing and the collective flourishing of women, nonbinary people, and marginalized communities.

At its core, healing within a community context means creating spaces where people can witness, support, and challenge each other to grow. It means finding or forming networks where emotional and spiritual health are prioritized and where everyone is encouraged to pursue liberation together. This work requires vulnerability but also leads to deep connection and accountability, allowing each person to be seen and heard without judgment.

Creating equitable relationships within these networks is a vital step in this process. Patriarchal systems have long driven the idea that competition, hierarchy, and control are necessary to build relationships. But we know from experience that these dynamics create distance, not closeness. True equity in relationships means embracing values like mutual respect, shared power, and compassionate accountability. It means rejecting patterns of dominance and submission and instead fostering environments where collaboration and shared responsibility are the foundation of every interaction.

So, how do we build these kinds of relationships? The first step is to recognize that equitable relationships require ongoing work—work that involves listening, reflecting, and adjusting behavior when necessary.

Focus on these four keys as you cultivate relationships that defy patriarchal oppression:

1. Shared Power and Mutual Respect

Equitable relationships are built on the understanding that everyone in the relationship has value and an equal voice. Whether it's in romantic partnerships, friendships, or community circles, creating balance in power dynamics is essential. This means recognizing when one person dominates the conversation or decisions and, instead, consciously trying to share power.

Imagine a relationship where everyone's opinions are valued, and no one feels the need to shrink themselves to maintain peace. When respect is mutual, and power is shared, there is room for everyone to show up fully as they are—without fear of being overshadowed or silenced.

2. Honoring Emotional Labor

Emotional labor is often disproportionately carried by women, nonbinary people, and marginalized communities, who are expected to provide emotional support while rarely receiving it in return. In equitable relationships, emotional labor is recognized, honored, and shared. This means being aware of how much emotional support is being asked of each person and ensuring that it does not always fall on one person's shoulders.

It's about reciprocity: listening as much as you speak, giving as much as you take, and making sure that each person feels supported. This also involves setting boundaries and communicating needs openly, without guilt or shame. In this way, we create nourishing and sustainable relationships for everyone involved.

3. Compassionate Accountability

Accountability is often framed as punitive, but equitable relationships are rooted in compassion and a shared commitment to growth. There will be times when patriarchal behaviors or unconscious biases show up, even in our most intentional spaces. What's important is how we handle these moments.

Compassionate accountability means addressing harmful behaviors with kindness and a desire to heal rather than with blame or punishment. It means holding space for each other to learn and grow while also being clear about what needs to change. In relationships built on equity, everyone commits to being accountable to their values and to each other, fostering a culture of transparency, trust, and mutual respect.

4. Creating Sacred Spaces for Healing and Growth

Equitable relationships flourish in environments where healing is prioritized. Gathering in circles, engaging in community activism, or simply creating time for deep, reflective conversations are all ways to build these spaces. Sacred spaces don't have to be formal—they can be as simple as regular check-ins with trusted friends or joining a group that shares your commitment to collective healing.

These spaces allow for the expression of emotions, the sharing of wisdom, and the celebration of each other's growth. They are places where you can rest, recharge, and be reminded that you are not walking this path alone. When we invest in building such spaces, we actively dismantle the isolating effects of patriarchy and create networks of support that uplift everyone.

Building Relationships That Reflect Your Values

Creating equitable relationships is not just about what we do in community spaces but also about how we bring these values into our everyday relationships. Whether it's with partners, friends, colleagues, or family members, living out the principles of equity and mutual respect is a practice that requires mindfulness and commitment. Here's how you can start:

- Be intentional with your time and energy. Consider where you're investing your emotional labor, and make sure that you're not overextending yourself to meet others' needs while neglecting your own.
- Communicate openly and honestly. Don't be afraid to have difficult conversations when necessary. Setting boundaries, sharing your needs, and addressing imbalances in relationships are all part of creating equitable connections.
- Celebrate each other's wins. Equitable relationships are not threatened by one person's success. Instead, they thrive on mutual encouragement. When one person grows or achieves something, everyone celebrates because the relationship is rooted in shared joy, not competition.

By committing to these practices, we can transform the way we relate to others and ourselves. We can build relationships that are not only nourishing and supportive but also revolutionary in their defiance of patriarchal norms.

The Role of Collective Healing

As we build equitable relationships, we must remember that healing is a collective journey. Liberation cannot happen in isolation—it requires us to work together, to support each other, and to hold space for the healing of both individuals and the community as a whole.

Community healing is especially powerful because it amplifies our capacity to grow. When we gather with others who share our values and our commitment to dismantling patriarchal systems, we create a ripple effect. One person's healing becomes the foundation for another's, and soon we find ourselves part of a larger movement toward collective liberation.

We are not meant to heal alone. By leaning into relationships that honor our worth, by creating spaces that nurture our growth, and by holding each other accountable with compassion, we become catalysts for change—not just in our own lives but in the world around us.

As you continue this journey of healing and empowerment, know that you are part of something much bigger than yourself. Each step you take toward building equitable relationships contributes to the larger movement of liberation and collective flourishing.

When we prioritize collective growth, we dismantle the isolating and individualistic values that patriarchy promotes. We begin to create resilient networks of support, care, and mutual aid in the face of oppression. Together, we can grow, heal, and flourish in ways that patriarchy has tried to prevent for far too long.

Final Words of Encouragement

As you close this book and continue your journey, remember that the path forward is one of liberation—not just for you, but for everyone. You are part of something much bigger than yourself, and every step you take toward healing and wholeness contributes to the creation of a world where all people are valued, all voices are heard, and all wisdom is honored.

Keep choosing this path. Keep trusting your intuition, honoring your emotions, and reclaiming your wisdom. Keep building relationships rooted in equity and mutual care. Most importantly, keep nourishing your spirit with practices that affirm your worth and remind you of the beauty of your journey.

Those of us who've embraced our inner old witch in the woods are rooting for you. Keep going. Never, ever give up on yourself.

The work you're doing is hard, but it's worth it. You are worth it. And the healed, equitable world you are helping create is worth it.

Acknowledgments

Torri, Megan, and Lisa, what a beautifully messy and fiery ride it's been (so far)! I am grateful for the conversations, memes, rants, creative jam sessions, and moments of deep grief we've shared. Thank you for embodying feminine wisdom, vulnerable courage, and fierce sisterhood.

Sharon Blackie, Dr. Clarissa Pinkola Estés, and Rabbi Tirzah Firestone—thank you for opening up my soul with volumes of story and feminine wisdom. From you, I learned that we are never truly separated from our ancestors, and some days, that's enough.

To my book chat peeps, I am grateful for our friendship and the safe space to discuss the highs and lows of writing.

Keely and Lisa, thank you for stewarding an overprotective author through the birth of this book. I look forward to many more years of changing the world together.

Tiffany, thanks for always having my back in this book-writing thing. I am grateful our paths crossed. You're forever my write-or-die girl!

My dudes, thank you for teaching me how to love and be loved. Being your momma has changed me for the better, which means you make the world a better place just by existing. Thanks also for all the cooking, dishes, and running errands you've done over the last few years. It has allowed me to heal, write, and encourage others to lean into their healing journey.

Last but not least, Gary, there's nothing like a road trip with you. I'm grateful we have miles to go before we sleep.

Notes

Chapter 1: The Feminine Wisdom Within

1 Barbara Ehrenreich and Deirdre English, *Witches, Midwives, & Nurses: A History of Women Healers* (Feminist Press at the City University of New York, 2010), 7.
2 Selena C. Baugh, "On Divinity and Marginalization: Western Christianity and African Spirituality as Impetuses of Gender In/Equality," *Perceptions* 5, no. 2 (2019), https://doi.org/10.15367/pj.v5i2.195.
3 Ana Navas-Acien, "The Colonial Roots of Violence Against Native American Women," Columbia University Mailman School of Public Health, March 16, 2023, https://tinyurl.com/2nb7wy5c.
4 Carlisle Indian School Digital Resource Center, "Teaching Resources," accessed January 14, 2025, https://tinyurl.com/582yk2ku.

Chapter 2: Bodies

1 Susan Akerman, "Asherah/Asherim: Bible," *Shalvi/Hyman Encyclopedia of Jewish Women*, February 27, 2009, https://tinyurl.com/568yfphe.
2 Augustine, *Augustine Sermons 184–229*, Wesley Scholar (n.d.), https://tinyurl.com/yu64czbw, 61.
3 Ambrose, *The Virgins* 2:2:6 (AD 377), quoted in "Mary: Without Sin," Church Fathers, 2025, https://tinyurl.com/mtdmkfcz.

4 Kevin Knight, "Church Fathers: The Perpetual Virginity of Mary (Jerome)," New Advent, accessed January 20, 2025, https://tinyurl.com/y8k8v3k3.
5 Merriam-Webster.com *Dictionary*, s.v., "Concupiscence," accessed January 20, 2025, https://tinyurl.com/5d68653y.
6 Augustine, *On Marriage and Concupiscence*, trans. Robert Ernest Wallis and Peter Holmes, https://tinyurl.com/55vadnph, chapter 27.
7 Dove, "New Dove Research Finds Beauty Pressures Up, and Women and Girls Calling for Change," Prnewswire.com, June 21, 2016, https://tinyurl.com/dbujpf76.
8 Rudy Volti, "The Organization of Work in Preindustrial Times," in *An Introduction to the Sociology of Work and Occupations*, 2nd ed. (Sage Publications, 2011), 19–23, https://tinyurl.com/mr2ckbyj.

Chapter 3: Mothering

1 Adrienne Rich, *Of Woman Born* (Norton, 2021), 25.
2 Elisabeth Badinter, *The Myth of Motherhood: An Historical View of the Maternal Instinct* (Souvenir Press, 1981), 30.
3 Badinter, *The Myth of Motherhood*, 73.

Chapter 4: Nourishing Self

1 NAACP, "Criminal Justice Fact Sheet," National Association for the Advancement of Colored People, May 24, 2021, https://tinyurl.com/ysb6y83y.
2 Quoted in Angela Saini, *Inferior: How Science Got Women Wrong and the New Research That's Rewriting the Story* (Beacon Press, 2017), 19.

Chapter 5: Pleasure

1 Emily Nagoski, host, *Come As You Are*, podcast, season 1, "Prelude: Pleasure Is the Measure," November 16, 2022, https://tinyurl.com/yxx4vtt5.
2 Kent C. Berridge and Morten L. Kringelbach, "Affective Neuroscience of Pleasure: Reward in Humans and Animals," *Psychopharmacology* 199, no. 3 (March 3, 2008): 457–480, https://doi.org/10.1007/s00213-008-1099-6.

Chapter 6: Feeling Things

1 Jacqueline S. Smith et al., "Constrained by Emotion: Women, Leadership, and Expressing Emotion in the Workplace," in *Handbook on Well-Being of Working Women*, ed. Mary Connerley and Jiyun Wu (Springer, 2016), https://doi.org/10.1007/978-94-017-9897-6_13.

2 Cecilia Tasca et al., "Women and Hysteria in the History of Mental Health," *Clinical Practice & Epidemiology in Mental Health* 8, no. 1 (October 19, 2012): 110–119, https://doi.org/10.2174/1745017901208010110.

3 "Charlotte Perkins Gilman," CT Women's Hall of Fame, accessed January 3, 2025, https://tinyurl.com/3e3ju7vj.

4 See https://angelajherrington.com/feeling-wheels.

Chapter 7: Governing Self

1 Marta Szastok, Małgorzata Kossowska, and Joanna Pyrkosz-Pacyna, "Women Can't Have It All: Benevolent Sexism Predicts Attitudes Toward Working (vs. Stay-at-Home) Mothers," *Social Psychological Bulletin* 14, no. 1 (May 15, 2019), https://doi.org/10.32872/spb.v14i1.29461.

2 Daniel A. Cox and Kelsey Eyre Hammond, "Young Women Are Leaving Church in Unprecedented Numbers," The Survey Center on American Life, April 4, 2024. https://tinyurl.com/2vk6vwe4.

3 Cox and Hammond, "Young Women Are Leaving Church in Unprecedented Numbers."

4 Britannica, "Beguines: Lay Religious Group," in *Encyclopædia Britannica*, December 30, 2019. https://tinyurl.com/2ufv984w.

5 "Haudenosaunee Guide for Educators," National Museum of the American Indian, 2009, https://tinyurl.com/5nby8a3x.

6 Carlos Almeida, "Beatriz Kimpa Vita and the Antonine Movement," in *Oxford Research Encyclopedia of African History*, October 22, 2024, https://doi.org/10.1093/acrefore/9780190277734.013.965.

7 Cox and Hammond, "Young Women Are Leaving Church in Unprecedented Numbers."

8 Kilgore, "Will Young Men Take over American Christianity?"

9 Heidi Keller, "Psychological Autonomy and Hierarchical Relatedness as Organizers of Developmental Pathways," *Philosophical Transactions of the Royal Society B: Biological Sciences* 371, no. 1686 (January 19, 2016): 20150070, https://doi.org/10.1098/rstb.2015.0070.

10 Sergio Sánchez-García et al., "Decreased Autonomy in Community-Dwelling Older Adults," *Clinical Interventions in Aging* 14

(November 2019): 2041–2053, https://doi.org/10.2147/cia.s225479.

11 Sánchez-García et al., "Decreased Autonomy in Community-Dwelling Older Adults."

12 Maria Compton, *Out of Faith* (Kings Road Publishing, 2024).

13 Katie Glass, "Maria Compton: 'I Escaped the Sect and My Kids Cut Me Off,'" *The Times*, August 11, 2024, https://tinyurl.com/3dr6ddk5.

14 Idayu Badilla Idris et al., "Women's Autonomy in Healthcare Decision Making: A Systematic Review," *BMC Women's Health* 23, no. 1 (December 2, 2023), https://doi.org/10.1186/s12905-023-02792-4.

15 Tanya Henry, "Access to Abortion and Women's Health: What the Research Shows," American Medical Association, July 5, 2022, https://tinyurl.com/3crpav62.

16 Danielle Brick et al., "Better to Decide Together: Shared Consumer Decision Making, Perceived Power, and Relationship Satisfaction," *Journal of Consumer Psychology* (2021): 32, https://doi.org/10.1002/jcpy.1260.

17 Carrie Blazina, "For American Couples, Gender Gaps in Sharing Household Responsibilities Persist amid Pandemic," Pew Research Center, January 25, 2021, https://tinyurl.com/ydjv25s7.

18 Isabel Fattal, "How Humans Handle Housework," *The Atlantic*, November 30, 2024, https://tinyurl.com/hsyufnbb.

Chapter 8: Leading

1 "2023 SBC Actions Regarding Women in Pastoral Ministry," SBC.net, 2023, https://tinyurl.com/yhymewb8.

2 Vatican, "Apostolic Letter, *Ordinatio Sacerdotalis* of John Paul II to the Bishops of the Catholic Church on Reserving Priestly Ordination to Men Alone," 1994, https://tinyurl.com/45enx6z2.

3 Angela J. Herrington, "5 Ways the Bible Supports Women Preaching," angelajherrington.com, May 21, 2021, https://tinyurl.com/5n7vttmz.

4 Junia Project, "Defusing the 1 Timothy 2:12 Bomb: What Does Paul Mean by Authority (Authentein)," The Junia Project, September 29, 2022, https://tinyurl.com/4saavhh9.

5 Sarah Pruitt, "How Early Church Leaders Downplayed Mary Magdalene's Influence by Calling Her a Whore," History, March 2019, https://tinyurl.com/39mxnv9n.

6 Herrington, "5 Ways the Bible Supports Women Preaching."

7 Arbora Johnson, "Phyllis Schlafly," National Women's History Museum, 2022, https://tinyurl.com/bdf2hk2a; Meghan Daum,

"Phyllis Schlafly: Back on the Attack," *Los Angeles Times*, March 31, 2011, https://tinyurl.com/3e7sf4n4.

8 LGBTIQA+ Greens, "Inclusion Is Not Erasure: Why TERF Ideology Harms the LGBTIQA+ Community," Green Party, January 30, 2021, https://tinyurl.com/59xxupu3.

Chapter 9: Wisdom

1 "4678. sophia," Bible Hub, accessed January 17, 2025, https://tinyurl.com/2tz6a7te.

2 "What Does It Mean to Trust in the Lord with All Your Heart (Proverbs 3:5)?," GotQuestions.org, accessed January 3, 2025, https://tinyurl.com/mwda77aj.

3 CBE International, "The Fundamentalist-Modernist Controversy and Women in Leadership," CBE International, November 2023, https://tinyurl.com/2z5t6bbs.

4 "Submission of Wives to Husbands," Focus on the Family, accessed January 3, 2025, https://tinyurl.com/jmzj2d6d.

Chapter 10: Aging

1 Clarissa Pinkola Estés, "Dr. Clarissa Pinkola Estés: Biography," accessed January 3, 2025, https://tinyurl.com/mry7ebft.

2 "The Power of the Crone," Maven Productions, July 25, 2018, https://tinyurl.com/24za4dw2.

3 Sharon Blackie and Stephen Jenkinson, "Eldering in the Age of Consumption," Dailygood.org, March 9, 2021, https://tinyurl.com/3jxre3u6.

Chapter 11: Reclaiming Your Roots

1 GoodReads, "A Quote by Arthur C. Clarke," www.goodreads.com, accessed January 3, 2025, https://tinyurl.com/4u3m9jcc.

2 Helen Thomson, "Study of Holocaust Survivors Finds Trauma Passed on to Children's Genes," *The Guardian*, August 21, 2015, https://tinyurl.com/4hes87v6.

3 Machiel Keestra, "Transgenerational Trauma and Worlded Brains: An Interdisciplinary Perspective on 'Post-Traumatic Slave Syndrome,'" *Worlding the Brain*, January 1, 2022, https://tinyurl.com/yc4f6wxw.

4 "Study Links Epigenetic Changes to Historic Trauma in Alaska Native Communities," ScienceDaily, September 7, 2023, https://tinyurl.com/42vc54zc.
5 See her website: https://www.tirzahfirestone.com/woundsintowisdom.
6 Tirzah Firestone, *Wounds into Wisdom* (Monkfish, 2019), 14.
7 https://angelajherrington.com/ancestors.

Bibliography

Akerman, Susan. "Asherah/Asherim: Bible." *Shalvi/Hyman Encyclopedia of Jewish Women*. February 27, 2009. https://tinyurl.com/568yfphe.

Almeida, Carlos. "Beatriz Kimpa Vita and the Antonine Movement." In *Oxford Research Encyclopedia of African History*, October 23, 2024. https://doi.org/10.1093/acrefore/9780190277734.013.965.

Anderson, Riana Elyse. "And Still We Rise: Parent–Child Relationships, Resilience, and School Readiness in Low-Income Urban Black Families." *Journal of Family Psychology* 32, no. 1 (February 2018): 60–70. https://doi.org/10.1037/fam0000348.

Augustine. *On Marriage and Concupiscence*. Translated by Robert Ernest Wallis and Peter Holmes. https://tinyurl.com/55vadnph.

Badinter, E. *The Myth of Motherhood: An Historical View of the Maternal Instinct*. Souvenir Press, 1981.

Baugh, Selena C. "On Divinity and Marginalization: Western Christianity and African Spirituality as Impetuses of Gender In/Equality." *Perceptions* 5, no. 2 (2019). https://doi.org/10.15367/pj.v5i2.195.

Berridge, Kent C., and Morten L. Kringelbach. "Affective Neuroscience of Pleasure: Reward in Humans and Animals." *Psychopharmacology* 199, no. 3 (March 3, 2008): 457–480. https://doi.org/10.1007/s00213-008-1099-6.

Blackie, Sharon, and Stephen Jenkinson. "Eldering in the Age of Consumption." Dailygood.org, March 9, 2021. https://tinyurl.com/3jxre3u6.

Blazina, Carrie. "For American Couples, Gender Gaps in Sharing Household Responsibilities Persist amid Pandemic." Pew Research Center, January 25, 2021. https://tinyurl.com/ydjv25s7.

Brick, Danielle, Lingrui Zhou, Tanya Chartrand, and Gavan Fitzsimons. "Better to Decide Together: Shared Consumer Decision Making, Perceived Power, and Relationship Satisfaction." *Journal of Consumer Psychology* 32 (2021). https://doi.org/10.1002/jcpy.1260.

Britannica, T. Editors of Encyclopaedia. “Beguines: Lay Religious Group.” *Encyclopædia Britannica*, December 30, 2019. https://tinyurl.com/2ufv984w.

Carlisle Indian School Digital Resource Center. “Teaching Resources.” Accessed January 14, 2025. https://tinyurl.com/582yk2ku.

CBE International. “The Fundamentalist-Modernist Controversy and Women in Leadership,” CBE International, November 2023. https://tinyurl.com/2z5t6bbs.

Church Fathers. “Mary: Without Sin.” Accessed January 20, 2025. https://tinyurl.com/mtdmkfcz.

Cox, Daniel A., and Kelsey Eyre Hammond. “Young Women Are Leaving Church in Unprecedented Numbers.” The Survey Center on American Life, April 4, 2024. https://tinyurl.com/2vk6vwe4.

CT Women’s Hall of Fame. “Charlotte Perkins Gilman.” Accessed January 3, 2025. https://tinyurl.com/3e3ju7vj.

Daum, Meghan. “Phyllis Schlafly: Back on the Attack.” *Los Angeles Times*, March 31, 2011. https://tinyurl.com/3e7sf4n4.

Dever, W. G. *Did God Have a Wife? Archaeology and Folk Religion in Ancient Israel*. Eerdmans, 2008.

Dove. “New Dove Research Finds Beauty Pressures Up, and Women and Girls Calling for Change.” Prnewswire.com, June 21, 2016. https://tinyurl.com/dbujpf76.

Ehrenreich, Barbara, and Deirdre English. *Witches, Midwives, & Nurses: A History of Women Healers*. Feminist Press at the City University of New York, 2010.

Estés, Clarissa Pinkola. “Dr. Clarissa Pinkola Estés: Biography.” Accessed January 3, 2025. https://tinyurl.com/mry7ebft.

Estés, Clarissa Pinkola. *Women Who Run with the Wolves*. Ballantine Books, 1992.

Every Child Thrives. “Recovering Stolen Lives and Histories from the Federal Indian Boarding School System.” Every Child Thrives, July 6, 2022. https://tinyurl.com/52n45u8r.

Fattal, Isabel. “How Humans Handle Housework.” *The Atlantic*, November 30, 2024. https://tinyurl.com/hsyufnbb.

Focus on the Family. “Submission of Wives to Husbands.” Accessed January 3, 2025. https://tinyurl.com/jmzj2d6d.

Glass, Katie. “Maria Compton: ‘I Escaped the Sect and My Kids Cut Me Off.’” *The Times*, August 11, 2024. https://tinyurl.com/3dr6ddk5.

GoodReads. “A Quote by Arthur C. Clarke.” Accessed January 3, 2025. https://tinyurl.com/4u3m9jcc.

GotQuestions.org. “What Does It Mean to Trust in the Lord with All Your Heart (Proverbs 3:5)?” Accessed January 3, 2025. https://tinyurl.com/mwda77aj.

Hamlin, Kimberly A. *From Eve to Evolution: Darwin, Science, and Women's Rights in Gilded Age America*. University of Chicago Press, 2014.

"Haudenosaunee Guide for Educators." National Museum of the American Indian, 2009. https://tinyurl.com/5nby8a3x.

Henry, Tanya. "Access to Abortion and Women's Health: What the Research Shows." American Medical Association, July 5, 2022. https://tinyurl.com/3crpav62.

Herrington, Angela J. "5 Ways the Bible Supports Women Preaching." angelajherrington.com, May 21, 2021. https://tinyurl.com/5n7vttmz.

Idris, Idayu Badilla, Amy Azira Hamis, Ayuzeity Bistari Md Bukhori, et al. "Women's Autonomy in Healthcare Decision Making: A Systematic Review." *BMC Women's Health* 23, no. 1 (December 2, 2023). https://doi.org/10.1186/s12905-023-02792-4.

Johnson, Arbora. "Phyllis Schlafly." National Women's History Museum, 2022. https://tinyurl.com/bdf2hk2a.

Junia Project. "Defusing the 1 Timothy 2:12 Bomb: What Does Paul Mean by Authority (Authentein)." The Junia Project, September 29, 2022. https://tinyurl.com/4saavhh9.

Keestra, Machiel. "Transgenerational Trauma and Worlded Brains: An Interdisciplinary Perspective on 'Post-Traumatic Slave Syndrome.'" Worlding the Brain, January 1, 2022. https://tinyurl.com/yc4f6wxw.

Keller, Heidi. "Psychological Autonomy and Hierarchical Relatedness as Organizers of Developmental Pathways." *Philosophical Transactions of the Royal Society B: Biological Sciences* 371, no. 1686 (January 19, 2016): 20150070. https://doi.org/10.1098/rstb.2015.0070.

Kilgore, Ed. "Will Young Men Take over American Christianity?" Intelligencer, September 24, 2024. https://tinyurl.com/yu4xsj4e.

Knight, Kevin. "Church Fathers: The Perpetual Virginity of Mary (Jerome)." New Advent, accessed January 20, 2025. https://tinyurl.com/y8k8v3k3.

LGBTIQA+ Greens. "Inclusion Is Not Erasure: Why TERF Ideology Harms the LGBTIQA+ Community." Green Party, January 30, 2021. https://tinyurl.com/59xxupu3.

Merriam-Webster.com Dictionary. s.v. "Concupiscence." Accessed January 20, 2025. https://tinyurl.com/5d68653y.

NAACP. "Criminal Justice Fact Sheet." National Association for the Advancement of Colored People, May 24, 2021. https://tinyurl.com/ysb6y83y.

Nagoski, Emily. *Come As You Are: The Surprising New Science That Will Transform Your Sex Life*, rev. and updated ed. Simon & Schuster, 2021.

Navas-Acien, Ana. "The Colonial Roots of Violence Against Native American Women." Columbia University Mailman School of Public Health, March 16, 2023. https://tinyurl.com/2nb7wy5c.

"Power of the Crone, The." Maven Productions, July 25, 2018. https://tinyurl.com/24za4dw2.

Pruitt, Sarah. "How Early Church Leaders Downplayed Mary Magdalene's Influence by Calling Her a Whore." History, March 2019. https://tinyurl.com/39mxnv9n.

Saini, Angela. *Inferior: How Science Got Women Wrong and the New Research That's Rewriting the Story.* Beacon Press, 2017.

Sánchez-García, Sergio, Carmen García-Peña, Eliseo Ramírez-García, Karla Moreno-Tamayo, and Guillermo Rafael Cantú-Quintanilla. "Decreased Autonomy in Community-Dwelling Older Adults." *Clinical Interventions in Aging* 14 (November 2019): 2041–2053. https://doi.org/10.2147/cia.s225479.

SBC. "2023 SBC Actions Regarding Women in Pastoral Ministry." SBC.net, 2023. https://tinyurl.com/yhymewb8.

Smith, Jacqueline S., Virginia L. Brescoll, and Erin L. Thomas. "Constrained by Emotion: Women, Leadership, and Expressing Emotion in the Workplace." In *Handbook on Well-Being of Working Women*, edited by Mary Connerley and Jiyun Wu. International Handbooks of Quality-of-Life. Springer, 2016. https://doi.org/10.1007/978-94-017-9897-6_13.

"Study Links Epigenetic Changes to Historic Trauma in Alaska Native Communities." ScienceDaily, September 7, 2023. https://tinyurl.com/42vc54zc.

Szastok, Marta, Małgorzata Kossowska, and Joanna Pyrkosz-Pacyna. "Women Can't Have It All: Benevolent Sexism Predicts Attitudes Toward Working (vs. Stay-at-Home) Mothers." *Social Psychological Bulletin* 14, no. 1 (May 15, 2019). https://doi.org/10.32872/spb.v14i1.29461.

Tasca, Cecilia, Mariangela Rapetti, Mauro Giovanni Carta, and Bianca Fadda. "Women and Hysteria in the History of Mental Health." *Clinical Practice & Epidemiology in Mental Health* 8, no. 1 (October 19, 2012): 110–119. https://doi.org/10.2174/1745017901208010110.

Thomson, Helen. "Study of Holocaust Survivors Finds Trauma Passed on to Children's Genes." *The Guardian*, August 21, 2015. https://tinyurl.com/4hes87v6.

Volti, Rudy. "The Organization of Work in Preindustrial Times." In *An Introduction to the Sociology of Work and Occupations*. 2nd ed. Sage Publications, 2011. https://tinyurl.com/mr2ckbyj.

Vatican. "Apostolic Letter, *Ordinatio Sacerdotalis* of John Paul II to the Bishops of the Catholic Church on Reserving Priestly Ordination to Men Alone." 1994. https://tinyurl.com/45enx6z2.